POCKET

W9-AYO-806

DEPRESSION GLASS

& MORE

1920s – 1960s

IDENTIFICATION AND VALUES

FIFTEENTH EDITION

Gene & Cathy Florence

Notice

The current values in this book should be used only as a guide. They are not intended to set prices, which vary from one section of the country to another. Auction prices as well as dealer prices vary greatly and are affected by condition as well as demand. Neither the authors nor the publisher assumes responsibility for any losses that might be incurred as a result of consulting this guide.

A listing of the colors to be found in each pattern is mentioned under each photo heading. However, the prices cataloged herein represent those colors most commonly collected in each pattern. See *Collector's Encyclopedia of Depression Glass* should you desire more detailed information.

Cover design by Beth Summers
Book design by Holly C. Long
Cover photography by Charles R. Lynch

Collector Books
P.O. Box 3009
Paducah, KY 42002 – 3009

Gene and Cathy Florence

P.O. Box 22186
Lexington, KY 40522

P.O. Box 64
Astatula, FL 34705

www.collectorbooks.com

Searching for a Publisher?

We are always looking for people knowledgeable within their fields. If you feel that there is a real need for a book on your collectible subject and have a large comprehensive collection, contact Collector Books.

Proudly printed and bound in the
United States of America

Preface

Depression glass as defined in this book is the colored glassware made primarily during the Depression years in the colors of amber, green, pink, blue, red, yellow, white, and crystal. There are other colors and some of the glassware included in this book was made later than the Depression era; but it has still been collected as that glassware because of its color. The main emphasis of this book is given to the inexpensively made glassware produced in quantity and sold through the five and dime stores or given away as premiums or included with the purchase of other products, e.g., spice shakers containing a certain brand spice.

Information for this book has come from over 2,350,000 miles of travel throughout the country in connection with glassware over the past 35 years and from the research and sale of over 1,150,000 copies of *Collector's Encyclopedia of Depression Glass*.

Acknowledgments

We would like at this time to say a word of thanks to the people who generously sent information and measurements to update listings in this book.

Also, a special thanks to our family for their support in various ways, gathering bits of information, taking over our household duties to leave us free to write.

Photography for this book was shared by Richard Walker and Charles R. Lynch. We wish to also thank the editorial staff of Collector Books for their work with the photography sessions and putting this book together.

Pricing

Glass that is in less than mint condition, i.e., chipped, cracked, scratched, or poorly molded, will bring very small prices unless extremely rare; and even then, it will bring only a tiny percentage of the price of glass that is in mint condition.

This book is meant as a guide to price; however, if your Depression glass comes to you at bargain rates or free from a relative, then that's all to the good!

Prices have become almost standardized due to national advertising by dealers and due to the Depression glass shows which are held from coast to coast. The advent of Internet auctions has made everyone aware of Depression glassware. However, there are some regional differences in prices due to glass being more readily available in some areas of the country than in others. Too, companies distributed certain pieces in some areas that they did not in others.

Contents

Contents

How to Find Depression Glass

The best place to find Depression glass is in your own basement, garage, or attic, or even in your own cupboards. Yes, that's true! Nearly everyone has at least a piece or two around their own home; it may be a bowl that belonged to grandmother and got handed down; it may be a complete setting that an aunt or someone got as a wedding gift and packed away for storage in the attic.

First of all, you need to learn to recognize the colors of Depression glass, for often the coloring of the glass is recognizable as Depression era glassware even when the pattern name is yet unknown. That was primarily the reason for making this a full-color book, so that the novice collector could acquaint himself with the full range of colors in which the glass may be found.

Once you have searched your own shelves and those of your immediate relatives and friends, your next source for finding Depression glass should be the garage sales, tag sales, yard sales, etc. where people are cleaning out their attics and garages. Don't forget the church bazaar, the Salvation Army store, or the Volunteers of America. You'll find competition is keen at these latter places; so, you'll need to shop early.

Now that you've covered all the aforementioned places, it's time to make a tour of the antique and junk shops in your area. These are often gold mines of the ridiculous to the sublime price-wise; have in mind what you'll pay for a particular item. Too, most of these shops expect to haggle a bit over price; don't be shy.

Household and estate auctions are often another valuable source for finding Depression glass, but it is wise to check out the merchandise before making a bid since chips and small damage to an item may be overlooked by the harried auctioneer.

Many collectors feel that antique shows and flea markets are the very best places to find Depression glass. Don't forget to put these on your agenda.

We find our best sources for finding particular pieces and patterns in Depression glass are the Depression glass shows held by clubs throughout the country. Don't forget to check the Internet if you have access to that. Internet auctions can prove to be fruitful places to shop. Find us at www.geneflorence.com.

Selling Depression Glass

One of the purposes of this book is to help you make money from any of your unwanted glassware. Any number of books imply that there are treasures in your attic, but few tell you how to reap benefits from them. Finding a reputable dealer in your area is not always an easy task, but here are a few suggestions. If you live in an area where a show is held regularly, watch for advertisements and attend the show. You might find a buyer for your glass among the dealers at the show. If there is a Depression glass club meeting in your area, there may be members there who would be willing to buy your glass or who could put you in contact with someone who would. The telephone directory or the ads under "Antiques" in your local newspaper may lead you to a dealer in glass who would be interested in buying yours; or you might take it to a local flea market and find a buyer among the dealers set up there.

The prices herein are retail and you can expect to receive 40 to 50% of the prices listed for the popular, highly collectible patterns, but only 20 to 25% of prices listed for the patterns that are not as avidly sought by collectors.

There are several factors a dealer will consider when offering for your piece: its condition, how popular this color is with potential buyers, whether or not the pattern is one numerous people collect, whether he has plenty in stock already, or whether he thinks he can make money on the piece before he's had to pack it up at 65 different shows throughout the country or dropped it and broken it. Popularity of a pattern and the demand for it are the two key factors in interesting a potential buyer of your glassware. This book should give you an accurate guide as to what to expect for your glass. You shouldn't be walking up to a dealer without the faintest idea of what your glass is worth; neither should you expect him to pay you retail price for the glass if you're sincerely wanting him to buy it.

What to Collect

Many beginning collectors make the mistake of trying to collect everything in sight. Unless you have a few oil wells on the side, you can soon find yourself out of funds doing this.

Our first suggestion is to study this book. Most of you have looked at the pictures before even starting to read this; that's a start. You have a general idea of what's available. Decide on one or possibly two patterns you like. Once you see it close at hand, you may change your mind; but that's all right. Collectors do that for a variety of reasons. However, it's wise to settle on something specific to look for rather than to pick and choose at random.

If money is a problem, peruse the prices of the various patterns and choose one that is less expensive to collect. However, you should become familiar with the whole range of patterns and you should have a general idea of the range of prices on the more expensive pieces of the patterns because everyone, sooner or later, stumbles onto a piece of glass worth $50.00 that's priced at $5.00. Even if you don't care for the piece or the pattern, you should go ahead and buy it because you'll either be able to trade it for the pattern you want, or you can sell it and use the extra money to buy the glass you like.

In the early 1960s through the early 1970s, you could buy Depression glass by the box and crate loads at auctions for a song; thus, you could afford to collect several patterns at once. However, those days have come to an end; so it's better to have something definite in mind to collect.

If money is no problem, then by all means, choose one of the more expensive patterns to collect. Since there are usually more people wanting these patterns, the market value for your pattern will be stable at the least, and will probably increase as the years pass.

Some people don't choose to collect an entire pattern. They collect one piece of every pattern, maybe plates for example. One California collector collects only cookie jars; another we know collects only candy jars; and there are numerous salt and pepper collections. You could choose to collect only one or two pieces of several patterns. In any case, you'll find the glass attractive to serve in and a real item of conversation.

If you are hard-bitten by the bug of collecting Depression glass, then you might possibly want a more detailed guide for the glass. Should that happen, we'd be delighted to recommend our *Collector's Encyclopedia of Depression Glass* or *Collectible Glassware of the '40s, '50s & '60s*, which can be ordered from this publisher or us. We receive letters daily from its delighted readers. In any case, happy hunting and finding. It's a hobby we think you'll not only enjoy, but one from which you might even profit.

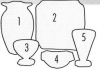

ADAM
Jeannette Glass Company, 1932 – 1934
pink, green, crystal, yellow, delphite
See Reproduction Section, Page 196

	Pink	Green		Pink	Green
Ashtray, 4½"	25.00	25.00	Plate, 6", sherbet	8.00	11.00
4 Bowl, 4¾", dessert	20.00	20.00	2 Plate, 7¾", sq. salad	18.00	16.00
Bowl, 5¾", cereal	60.00	50.00	Plate, 9", sq. dinner	32.00	30.00
Bowl, 7¾"	26.00	28.00	Plate, 9", grill	26.00	23.00
Bowl, 9", covered	70.00	95.00	Platter, 11¾"	30.00	33.00
Bowl, 10", oval	35.00	40.00	Relish dish, 8", divided	20.00	25.00
Butter dish & cover	100.00	365.00	Salt & pepper, 4"	90.00	115.00
Cake plate, 10", footed	28.00	30.00	Saucer, sq. 6"	6.00	7.50
Candlesticks, 4", pr.	100.00	125.00	3 Sherbet, 3"	28.00	35.00
Candy jar & cover, 2½"	125.00	125.00	Sugar	20.00	20.00
Coaster, 3¾"	22.00	20.00	Sugar/candy cover	25.00	45.00
Creamer	25.00	28.00	5 Tumbler, 4½"	30.00	28.00
Cup	28.00	25.00	Tumbler, 5½", iced tea	75.00	70.00
Lamp	495.00	495.00	1 Vase, 7½"	495.00	125.00
Pitcher, 8", 32 oz.	45.00	45.00			

ADAM'S RIB
Line #900, Diamond Glassware Co., circa 1925

amber, blue, green, pink; some marigold, milk and crystal with marigold iridescence, vaseline; and colors decorated with gold, silver, white enamel, florals; and flashed colors of blue and orange with black trim

	Non-Iridescent	Iridescent
Base, black, pedestal, 3-toe (for flat bowls)	15.00	——
1 Bowl, vegetable, flared (belled) rim	60.00	——
Bowl, flat, rolled edge	40.00	——
Bowl, console, pedestal foot	55.00	175.00
Bowl, 8", 3-footed, salad	45.00	——
Candy, 3-footed bonbon with lid	45.00	——
Candy, oval, flat	65.00	——
6 Candy, footed jar & cover	55.00	——
Candle, blown	30.00	——
3 Candle, tall	32.00	——
Cigarette holder, footed	25.00	——
Compote, cheese, non-ribbed	25.00	——
2 Comport, sm.	35.00	——
Comport, 6½" tall	40.00	80.00
Comport, lg. fruit	60.00	100.00
4 Cup	18.00	——

	Non-Iridescent	Iridescent
Creamer	25.00	45.00
5 Mayonnaise, 6" with ladle	45.00	——
Mug (or lemonade)	30.00	90.00
Pitcher, lemonade, applied hndl.	175.00	350.00
Plate, dessert	10.00	——
Plate, lunch	18.00	——
Plate, cracker, with center rim	30.00	——
Saucer	6.00	——
Sandwich, center flat top hndl.	——	50.00
Sandwich, center ½ hex hndl.	30.00	55.00
Sherbet, flat rim	20.00	——
Sugar, open	25.00	45.00
Tray, oval sugar/creamer (8½" x 6¼")	20.00	35.00
Vase, fan	40.00	65.00
Vase, 8½", footed, flare rim	75.00	110.00
Vase, 9¾"	95.00	150.00

"ADDIE," "TWELVE POINT"
Line #34, New Martinsville Glass Mfg. Co., circa 1930
black, crystal, cobalt, green, jade green satin, pink, red; and with Lotus Glass Co. silver decoration

	Jade/Red Black/ Cobalt	All Other Colors		Jade/Red Black/ Cobalt	All Other Colors
Bowl, lg. flare rim, vegetable	45.00	35.00	9 Sandwich tray, 2 hndl.	32.00	22.00
Candlestick, 3½"	25.00	20.00	4 Saucer	3.00	2.00
7 Creamer, footed	15.00	12.00	Saucer, demi	5.00	
Cup, demi	15.00	—	2 Sherbet, footed	15.00	8.00
3 Cup, footed	12.00	8.00	8 Sugar, open, footed	15.00	8.00
Mayonnaise, 5"	30.00	15.00	Tumbler, footed, 6 oz., juice	15.00	8.00
1 Plate, lunch	12.50	8.00	Tumbler, footed, 9 oz., water	18.00	12.00

AMERICAN PIONEER
Liberty Works, 1931 – 1934
pink, green, amber, crystal

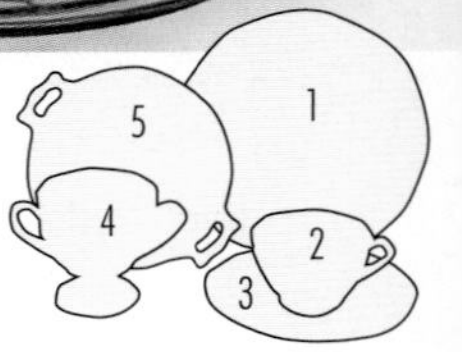

	Pink	Green
Bowl, 5", hndl.	25.00	25.00
Bowl, 8¾", covered	125.00	165.00
Bowl, 9", hndl.	30.00	38.00
Bowl, console, 10¾"	60.00	70.00
Candlesticks, 6½", pr.	110.00	135.00
Candy jar & cover, 1 lb.	95.00	110.00
Candy jar & cover, 1½ lb.	100.00	135.00
Cheese & cracker set (indented platter & compote)	60.00	70.00
Coaster, 3½"	30.00	30.00
Creamer, 2¾"	25.00	20.00
Creamer, 3½"	20.00	22.00
2 Cup	12.00	12.00
Dresser set (2 colognes, powder jar, on indented 7½" tray)	495.00	495.00
Goblet, wine, 4", 3 oz.	40.00	55.00
Goblet, water, 6", 8 oz.	50.00	60.00
Ice bucket, 6"	60.00	70.00
Lamp, 8½" tall	135.00	165.00

	Pink	Green
Mayonnaise, 4¼"	60.00	90.00
Pitcher, 5", covered urn	175.00	225.00
Pitcher, 7", covered urn	195.00	250.00
Plate, 6",	12.50	15.00
5 Plate, 6", hndl.	12.50	15.00
1 Plate, 8"	14.00	14.00
Plate, 11½", hndl.	30.00	40.00
3 Saucer	5.00	5.00
Sherbet, 3½"	16.00	20.00
Sherbet, 4¾"	40.00	45.00
Sugar, 2¾"	20.00	22.00
4 Sugar, 3½"	20.00	22.00
Tumbler, 5 oz., juice	40.00	45.00
Tumbler, 4", 8 oz.	40.00	55.00
Tumbler, 5", 12 oz.	50.00	65.00
Vase, 7", four styles, rolled or crimped edge, straight	120.00	145.00
Whiskey, 2¼", 2 oz.	50.00	100.00

AMERICAN SWEETHEART
MacBeth-Evans Glass Company, 1930 – 1936
pink, monax, cremax, red, and blue

	Pink	Monax
Bowl, 3¾", flat, berry	80.00	——
Bowl, 4½", cream soup	80.00	110.00
Bowl, 6", cereal	16.00	18.00
Bowl, 9", round, berry	50.00	65.00
4 Bowl, 9½", flat soup	72.00	85.00
Bowl, 11", oval vegetable	65.00	80.00
Bowl, 18", console	——	495.00
5 Creamer, footed	13.00	10.00
6 Cup	16.00	8.00
Pitcher, 60 oz.	1,050.00	——
Pitcher, 80 oz.	795.00	——
2 Plate, 6", bread & butter	6.00	6.50
Plate, 8", salad	12.00	9.00
Plate, 9", luncheon	——	12.00

	Pink	Monax
1 Plate, 9¾" – 10¼", dinner	32.00	26.00
Plate, 12", salver	25.00	21.00
Plate, 15½"	——	250.00
Platter, 13", oval	50.00	65.00
Salt & pepper, footed	595.00	450.00
7 Saucer	3.00	2.00
Sherbet, footed, 3¾"	23.00	——
Sherbet, footed, 4¼"	19.00	22.00
3 Sugar, open, footed	14.50	8.00
Sugar cover	——	500.00
Tumbler, 3½", 5 oz	90.00	——
Tumbler, 4¼", 9 oz.	85.00	——
Tumbler, 4¾", 10 oz.	135.00	——

ANNIVERSARY
Jeannette Glass Company, 1947 – 1949
pink; late 1960s – mid 1970s in crystal and iridescent

	Crystal	Pink
Bowl, 4⅞", berry	5.00	10.00
Bowl, 7⅜", soup	7.00	17.50
Bowl, 9", fruit	12.00	30.00
Butter dish & cover	30.00	60.00
5 Candle	9.00	
2 Candy jar & cover	30.00	55.00
Cake plate, 12½"	14.00	20.00
Cake plate with cover	18.00	—
Compote, open, 3-legged	5.00	15.00
Creamer, footed	4.00	12.00
3 Cup	3.00	9.00
Pickle dish, 9"	6.00	18.00

	Crystal	Pink
Plate, 6¼", sherbet	2.00	4.00
1 Plate, 9", dinner	6.00	15.00
Plate, 12½", sandwich server	11.00	23.00
Relish dish, 8"	8.00	15.00
7 Saucer	1.00	2.00
6 Sherbet, footed	4.00	11.00
4 Sugar	3.00	9.00
8 Sugar cover	4.00	11.00
Vase, 6½"	16.00	30.00
Vase, wall pin-up	20.00	40.00
Wine glass, 2½ oz.	10.00	18.00

AUNT POLLY
U.S. Glass Company, late 1920s
green, blue, iridescent

	Green	Blue		Green	Blue
3 Bowl, 4⅜", berry	6.00	14.00	Pitcher, 8", 48 oz.	——	225.00
Bowl, 4¾", 2" high	16.00	——	Plate, 6", sherbet	5.00	10.00
Bowl, 5½", 1 hndl.	15.00	25.00	Plate, 8", luncheon	——	18.00
2 Bowl, 7¼", oval, hndl., pickle	10.00	30.00	Salt & pepper	——	250.00
Bowl, 7⅞", lg. berry	18.00	45.00	Sherbet	10.00	10.00
Bowl, 8⅜", oval	75.00	150.00	1 Sugar	25.00	35.00
Butter dish & cover	225.00	200.00	1 Sugar cover	60.00	165.00
4 Candy, cover, 2 hndl.	65.00	90.00	Tumbler, 3⅝", 8 oz.	——	30.00
Candy, footed, 2 hndl.	30.00	60.00	Vase, 6½", footed	35.00	55.00
Creamer	35.00	60.00			

AURORA
Hazel Atlas Company, 1937 – 1938
cobalt, pink, green

	Cobalt
4 Bowl, 4½"	62.00
1 Bowl, 5⅜"	16.00
2 Creamer, 4½"	25.00
5 Cup	15.00

	Cobalt
Plate, 6½"	10.00
6 Saucer	4.00
7 Tumbler, 4¾"	25.00

AVOCADO, "SWEET PEAR," No. 601
Indiana Glass Company, 1923 – 1933
pink, green, crystal, white
See Reproduction Section, Page 197

	Pink	Green		Pink	Green
Bowl, 5¼", 2 hndl.	30.00	33.00	1 Pitcher, 64 oz.	950.00	1,400.00
Bowl, 6", relish, footed	28.00	30.00	Plate, 6¾", sherbet	14.00	16.00
Bowl, 7", preserve, 1 hndl.	28.00	30.00	2 Plate, 8¼", luncheon	17.00	20.00
Bowl, 7½", salad	50.00	70.00	Plate, 10½", 2 hndl. cake	50.00	60.00
Bowl, 8", oval, 2 hndl.	30.00	35.00	6 Saucer	20.00	20.00
Bowl, 9½", 3¼" deep	150.00	180.00	4 Sherbet	55.00	70.00
Creamer, footed	32.00	35.00	7 Sugar, footed	32.00	35.00
Cup, footed	32.00	35.00	Tumbler, ftd.	260.00	335.00

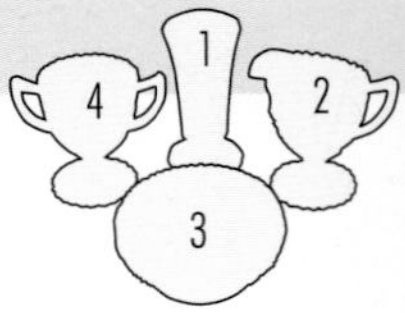

BEADED BLOCK
Imperial Glass Company, 1927 – 1930s
pink, green, crystal, ice blue, vaseline, iridescent, amber, opalescent colors

	Green	Opalescent		Green	Opalescent
Bowl, 4½", 2 hndl. jelly	20.00	45.00	Bowl, 7½", round, plain edge	30.00	45.00
3 Bowl, 4½", round, lily	20.00	45.00	Bowl, 8¼", celery	38.00	60.00
Bowl, 5½", sq.	20.00	35.00	2 Creamer	25.00	50.00
Bowl, 5½", 1 hndl.	30.00	40.00	Pitcher, 5¼", pint jug	90.00	250.00
Bowl, 6" deep, round	25.00	40.00	Plate, 7¾" sq.	22.00	35.00
Bowl, 6¼", round	25.00	40.00	Plate, 8¾", round	30.00	45.00
Bowl, 6½", round	25.00	40.00	Stemmed jelly, 4½"	25.00	38.00
Bowl, 6½", 2 hndl. pickle	30.00	50.00	Stemmed jelly, 4½", flared top	25.00	40.00
Bowl, 6¾", round, unflared	25.00	60.00	4 Sugar	25.00	50.00
Bowl, 7¼", round, flared	30.00	50.00	1 Vase, 6", bouquet	25.00	55.00
Bowl, 7½", round, fluted edges	30.00	50.00			

BEADED EDGE
Westmoreland Glass Company, late 1930s – 1950s
pattern #22 Milk Glass

	Plain	Decorated		Plain	Decorated
Creamer, footed	10.00	17.50	Plate, 15", torte	32.00	65.00
Creamer, footed with lid, #108	20.00	38.00	Platter, 12", oval with tab handles	35.00	125.00
2 Cup	5.00	12.00	Relish, 3-part	30.00	110.00
Nappy, 5"	4.50	15.00	Salt & pepper, pr.	30.00	90.00
Nappy, 6", crimped, oval	7.00	25.00	3 Saucer	2.00	3.00
Plate, 6", bread & butter	5.00	10.00	Sherbet, footed	9.00	15.00
Plate, 7", salad	7.00	16.00	Sugar, footed	10.00	17.50
Plate, 8½", luncheon	5.00	10.00	Sugar, footed with lid #108	18.00	38.00
Plate, 10½", dinner	14.00	40.00	Tumbler, 8 oz., footed	10.00	16.00

"BERLIN," "REEDED WAFFLE"
Line #124, Westmoreland Speciality Co., circa 1924
blue, crystal, green, pink; ruby circa 1980s

	Crystal*
3 Basket	27.50
Bowl, bonbon, 1 hndl	15.00
Bowl, 6½", round	15.00
Bowl, sq.	22.00
4 Bowl, 2 hndl. cream soup	20.00
Bowl, 7", round	20.00
Bowl, 7½", round	25.00
6 Bowl, oval, pickle	22.50

	Crystal*
1 Creamer	18.00
Mayonnaise & liner	30.00
2 Pitcher	75.00
Plate, 9", lunch	15.00
5 Sugar	15.00
Tray, 2 hndl., celery	27.50
Vase, footed	35.00

*Double price of crystal for colors.

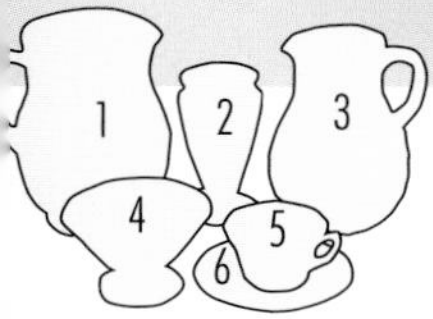

BLOCK OPTIC, "BLOCK"
Hocking Glass Company, 1929 – 1933
green, yellow, pink, crystal

	Pink	Green
Bowl, 4¼", berry	12.00	8.00
Bowl, 5¼", cereal	28.00	13.00
Bowl, 7¼", salad	160.00	140.00
Bowl, 8½", lg. berry	35.00	40.00
Butter dish & cover, 3"x5"	——	50.00
Candlesticks, 1¾", pr.	70.00	100.00
Candy jar & cover, 2¼" tall	60.00	60.00
Candy jar cover, 6¼" tall	150.00	60.00
4 Compote, 4" wide mayonnaise	95.00	75.00
Creamer, three styles: cone shaped, round footed & flat	15.00	13.00
5 Cup, four styles	7.00	7.00
Goblet, 4", cocktail	40.00	40.00
Goblet, 4½", wine	45.00	40.00
Goblet, 5¾", 9 oz.	30.00	28.00
Ice bucket	90.00	40.00
Ice tub or butter tub, open	125.00	65.00
Mug, flat creamer, no spout	——	40.00
3 Pitcher, 7⅝", 54 oz., bulbous	495.00	95.00
1 Pitcher, 8½", 54 oz.	55.00	65.00
Pitcher, 8", 80 oz.	165.00	105.00
Plate, 6", sherbet	3.00	3.00

	Pink	Green
Plate, 8", luncheon	8.00	7.00
Plate, 9", dinner	37.50	27.50
Salt & pepper, footed	95.00	45.00
Salt & pepper, squatty	——	120.00
Sandwich server, center hndl.	75.00	75.00
6 Saucer, 2 sizes, cup ring	7.00	8.00
Sherbet, non-stemmed (cone)	——	3.00
Sherbet, 3¼", 5½ oz.	7.50	6.00
Sherbet, 4¾", 6 oz.	17.00	16.00
Sugar, three styles: same as creamer.	12.50	12.50
Tumbler, 3½", 5 oz., flat	28.00	25.00
Tumbler, 3¼", 3 oz., footed	30.00	30.00
Tumbler, 9½ oz., flat	15.00	15.00
Tumbler, 9 oz., footed	17.00	20.00
Tumbler, 10 oz., flat	18.00	20.00
Tumbler, 6", 10 oz., footed	38.00	35.00
Tumbler, 15 oz., flat	55.00	55.00
Tumble-up night set: 3", tumbler bottle & tumbler, 6" high	——	85.00
2 Vase, 5¾", blown	——	350.00
Whiskey, 2¼", 2 oz.	35.00	32.00

21

"BOWKNOT"
Unknown Manufacturer
green

	Green
6 Bowl, 4½", berry	28.00
4 Bowl, 5½", cereal	38.00
7 Cup	10.00
2 Plate, 6¾", salad	15.00

	Green
5 Sherbet, low footed	23.00
1 Tumbler, 5", 10 oz.	28.00
3 Tumbler, 5", 10 oz., footed	25.00

"BUBBLE," "FIRE KING"
Hocking Glass Company, 1941 – 1965
blue, dark green, ruby red, crystal

	Crystal	Blue
Bowl, 4", berry	4.00	18.00
Bowl, 4¼", fruit	4.00	14.00
Bowl, 5¼", cereal	10.00	14.00
Bowl, 7¾", flat soup	12.00	15.00
Bowl, 8⅜", lg. berry	10.00	16.00
Creamer	6.00	35.00
2 Cup	3.00	4.00
1 Pitcher, 64 oz., ice lip	125.00	40.00*
Plate, 6¾", bread & butter	3.00	—
Plate, 9⅜", grill	—	22.00

* Red

	Crystal	Blue
6 Plate, 9⅜", dinner	7.00	7.00
Platter, 12", oval	15.00	16.00
3 Saucer	1.00	1.25
Sugar	6.00	25.00
4 Tumbler, 5 oz., juice	3.50	8.00*
Tumbler, 8 oz., 3¼", old fashioned	10.00	16.00
Tumbler, 9 oz., water	5.00	9.00*
5 Tumbler, 12 oz., iced tea	12.00	12.00*
Tumbler, 16 oz., lemonade	14.00	16.00*

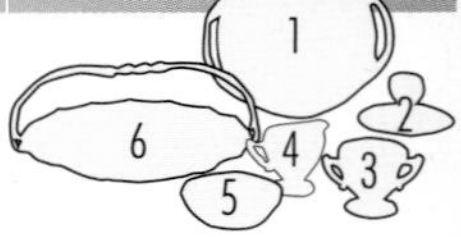

CAMELLIA
Jeannette Glass Company, 1950s
crystal, crystal with gold trim, iridized, flashed red or blue

	Crystal
5 Bowl, 5"	6.00
Bowl, 1 hndl., nappy	9.00
Bowl, 87/8", vegetable	12.00
Bowl, 9⅜", 4¼" deep, punch	18.00
Bowl, 10⅛", 3½" deep, salad	18.00
2 Candleholder	12.00
4 Creamer, footed	7.50
Cup	2.00

	Crystal
6 Plate, 8⅜", luncheon	6.00
Plate, 12", sandwich	12.00
Relish, 6¾" x 11¾"	14.00
Saucer	.50
3 Sugar, footed	7.50
Tidbit, 2-tier	20.00
1 Tray, 2 hndl., 8¼"	16.00

CAMEO, "BALLERINA," or "DANCING GIRL"
Hocking Glass Company, 1930 – 1934
green, yellow, pink, and crystal with a platinum rim

	Green	Yellow		Green	Yellow
Bowl, 4¾", cream soup	165.00	—	Decanter, 10" with stopper	215.00	—
Bowl, 5½", cereal	30.00	30.00	Decanter, 10" with stopper, frosted (stoppers		
Bowl, 7¼", salad	70.00	—	represent ½ value of decanter)	40.00	—
Bowl, 8¼", lg. berry	45.00	—	Domino tray, 7", with 3" indentation	225.00	—
Bowl, 9", rimmed soup	75.00	—	Goblet, 3½", wine	1,000.00	—
Bowl, 10", oval vegetable	30.00	40.00	Goblet, 4", wine	72.00	—
Bowl, 11", 3-leg console	90.00	125.00	Goblet, 6", water	67.50	—
3 Butter dish & cover	235.00	1,500.00	Ice bowl or open butter		
Cake plate, 10", 3 legs	20.00	—	3" tall x 5½" wide	210.00	—
Candlesticks, 4", pr.	120.00	—	Jam jar, 2" & cover	250.00	—
Candy jar, low 4", cover	90.00	115.00	Pitcher, 5¾", syrup or milk, 20 oz.	320.00	1,500.00
Candy jar, 6½" tall & cover	205.00	—	Pitcher, 6", juice, 36 oz.	75.00	—
Cocktail shaker (metal lid) appears in			Pitcher, 8½", water, 56 oz.	70.00	—
crystal only	—	750.00	Plate, 6", sherbet	4.00	3.00
5 Compote, 4" wide mayonnaise	45.00	—	1 Plate, 8", luncheon	10.00	10.00
Cookie jar & cover	60.00	—	Plate, 8½", sq.	50.00	250.00
Creamer, 3¼"	22.00	17.00	Plate, 9½", dinner	18.00	11.00
Creamer, 4¼"	30.00	—	Plate, 10", sandwich	18.00	—
Cup, 2 styles	12.00	9.00	Plate, 10½", grill	15.00	9.00

Continued

CAMEO, "BALLERINA," OR "DANCING GIRL"

	Green	Yellow
Plate, 10½", grill, closed hndl.	75.00	6.00
Plate, 10½", closed hndl.	16.00	12.00
Platter, 12", closed hndl.	28.00	38.00
Relish, 3-part, 7½", footed	30.00	——
Salt & pepper, footed, pr.	75.00	——
Sandwich server, center hndl.	6,000.00	——
Saucer with cup ring	250.00	——
Saucer, 6" (sherbet plate)	4.00	3.00
2 Sherbet, 3⅛"	15.00	40.00
4 Sherbet, 4⅞"	30.00	90.00
Sugar, 3¼"	18.00	16.00
Sugar, 4¼"	30.00	——

	Green	Yellow
Tumbler, 3¾", juice, 5 oz.	35.00	——
Tumbler, 4", water, 9 oz.	30.00	——
Tumbler, 4¾", flat, 10 oz.	30.00	——
Tumbler, 5", flat, 11 oz.	35.00	110.00
Tumbler, 5¼", 15 oz.	80.00	350.00
Tumbler, footed juice, 3 oz.	75.00	——
Tumbler, 5", footed, 9 oz.	30.00	18.00
Tumbler, 5¾", footed, 11 oz.	75.00	——
Vase, 5¾"	310.00	——
Vase, 8"	65.00	——
Water bottle (dark green) Whitehouse vinegar	25.00	——

5

CAPRI, "SEASHELL," "SWIRL COLONIAL," "COLONIAL, "ALPINE"

Hazel Ware, Division of Continental Can, 1960s

blue

	Blue
Ashtray, 3¼", triangular or round	6.00
Ashtray, 3½", sq., embossed flower	17.50
Ashtray, 5", round	8.00
Ashtray, 6⅞", triangular	12.00
Bowl, 4¾", octagonal	7.00
Bowl, 4¾", swirled	6.00
Bowl, 4⅞", round, "dots"	5.00
Bowl, 5⅜", salad, round, "hobnails"	7.00
Bowl, 5⅝" "Colony Swirl"	8.00
Bowl, 5¾", sq., deep, Colony	10.00
Bowl, 6", round, tulip	10.00
Bowl, 6", round, "dots"	7.00
2 Bowl, 6", round, sq. bottom, Colony	7.00
Bowl, 6 1/16", round, "Colony Swirl"	7.00
Bowl, 7¾", oval, Colony	15.00
Bowl, 7¾", rectangular, Colony	14.00
Bowl, 8¾", swirled	12.00
Bowl, 9⅛" x 3" high	25.00
Bowl, 9½" x 2⅞" high	22.00
Bowl, 9½" oval 1½" high	9.00
Bowl, 10¾", salad, Colony	24.00
1 Candy jar, with cover, footed	32.00
Chip & dip, 8¾" and 4¾" swirled bowls on metal rack	25.00
Creamer, round	12.50
3 Cup, octagonal	4.00
Cup, round, "dots" or swirled	4.00
Cup, round, tulip	7.00
Plate, 5¾", bread & butter, octagonal	4.00
Plate, 7", salad, round, "Colony Swirl"	7.00
Plate, 7⅛", round, salad, "Colony Swirl"	7.00
Plate, 7¼", salad, "hobnails" or octagonal	6.00

	Blue
Plate, 8", sq. with or without sq. cup rest	8.00
Plate, 8⅞", sq.	10.00
Plate, 8⅞", sq., with round cup rest	9.00
Plate, 9½", round, snack with cup rest, tulip	9.50
Plate, 9¾", dinner, octagonal	9.00
Plate, 9⅞", dinner, round, "hobnails"	8.00
Plate, 10", snack, fan shaped with cup rest	7.00
Saucer, 5½", sq.	1.00
Saucer, 6", round, "hobnails"	1.00
4 Saucer, octagonal	1.00
Stem, 4½", sherbet	7.50
5 Stem, 5½", water	9.00
Sugar with lid, round	20.00
Tidbit, 3-tier (9⅞" plate, 7⅛" plate, 6" saucer)	22.50
Tumbler, 2¾", 4 oz., "Colony Swirl"	7.00
Tumbler, 3", 4 oz., fruit "dots"	4.00
Tumbler, 3", 5 oz., pentagonal bottom	7.00
Tumbler, 3 1/16", Colony or "Colony Swirl"	8.00
Tumbler, 3⅛", 5 oz., pentagonal	7.00
Tumbler, 3¼", 8 oz., old fashioned, "dots"	8.00
Tumbler, 3⅝", 3 oz., "dots"	4.00
Tumbler, 4", "dots"	4.00
Tumbler, 4¼", 9 oz., "Colony Swirl"	7.50
Tumbler, 4¼", 9 oz., water, pentagonal bottom	7.50
Tumbler, 5", 12 oz., "Colony Swirl"	10.00
Tumbler, 5", 12 oz., tea, pentagonal bottom	10.00
Tumbler, 5¼", "dots"	5.00
Tumbler, 5½", 12 oz., tea, swirl	10.00
Tumbler, 6", 10 oz., "dots"	7.00
Vase, 8", "dots"	20.00
Vase, 8½", ruffled	30.00

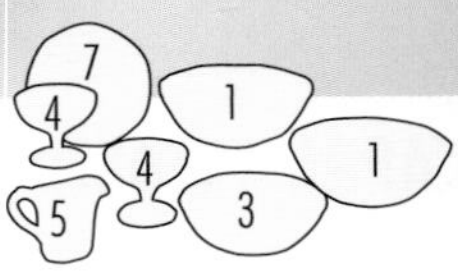

CHERRYBERRY
U.S. Glass Company, 1928 – 1931
pink, green, iridescent

	Pink or Green
Bowl, 4", berry	15.00
3 Bowl, 6¼", 2" deep	120.00
1 Bowl, 6½" deep, berry	25.00
Butter dish & cover	190.00
Compote, 5¾"	28.00
5 Creamer, sm.	20.00
Creamer, lg., 4⅝"	35.00
Olive dish, 5", 1 hndl.	20.00
Pickle dish	20.00

	Pink or Green
Pitcher, 7¾"	195.00
7 Plate, 6", sherbet	12.00
Plate, 7½", salad	16.00
4 Sherbet	10.00
Sugar, sm., open	22.00
Sugar, lg.	20.00
Sugar cover	50.00
Tumbler, 3⅝", 9 oz.	35.00

CHERRY BLOSSOM
Jeannette Glass Company, 1930 – 1939
pink, green, delphite, crystal
See Reproduction Section, Pages 198 – 201

	Pink	Green
Bowl, 4¾", berry	14.00	18.00
Bowl, 5¾", cereal	50.00	45.00
Bowl, 7¾", flat soup	110.00	95.00
Bowl, 8½", round berry	50.00	50.00
Bowl, 9", oval vegetable	55.00	50.00
Bowl, 9", 2 hndl.	50.00	75.00
Bowl, 10½", 3-leg fruit	95.00	100.00
Butter dish & cover	100.00	120.00
Cake plate (3 legs) 10¼"	35.00	40.00
Coaster	12.00	13.00
Creamer	20.00	23.00
4 Cup	16.00	18.00
Mug, 7 oz.	450.00	450.00
Pitcher, 6¾", AOP, 36 oz., scalloped or round bottom	75.00	65.00
Pitcher, 8", PAT, 36 oz., footed	75.00	75.00
2 Pitcher, 8", PAT, 42 oz., flat	80.00	80.00
Plate, 6", sherbet	7.00	9.00
Plate, 7", salad	24.00	21.00
1 Plate, 9", dinner	20.00	22.00
Plate, 9", grill	30.00	30.00
Platter, 9", oval	950.00	1,100.00
Platter, 11", oval	48.00	50.00

	Pink	Green
Platter, 13" & 13", divided	75.00	80.00
Salt & pepper, scalloped	1,300.00	1,100.00
5 Saucer	3.00	4.00
Sherbet	17.00	20.00
6 Sugar	14.00	15.00
7 Sugar cover	20.00	20.00
Tray, 10½", sandwich, 2 hndl.	30.00	35.00
Tumbler, 3¾", 4 oz., footed AOP, round	18.00	22.00
Tumbler, 4½", 9 oz., round foot AOP	35.00	35.00
Tumbler, 4½", 8 oz., scalloped foot AOP	35.00	35.00
3 Tumbler, 3½", 4 oz., flat PAT	25.00	30.00
Tumbler, 4¼", 9 oz., flat PAT	18.00	21.00
Tumbler, 5", 12 oz., flat PAT	75.00	85.00

CHILD'S JUNIOR DINNER SET

	Pink
Creamer	40.00
Sugar	40.00
Original box	35.00
Plate, 6"	10.00
Cup	30.00
Saucer	5.00
14-pc. set	295.00

29

CHINEX CLASSIC
MacBeth-Evans Division of Corning Glass Works, late 1930s – early 1940s
ivory, ivory decorated

	Ivory	Decorated
4 Bowl, 5¾", cereal	5.00	18.00
Bowl, 6¾", salad	12.00	40.00
Bowl, 7", vegetable	14.00	40.00
Bowl, 7¾", flat soup	12.50	40.00
Bowl, 9", vegetable	10.00	40.00
Butter dish	40.00	55.00
Creamer	5.00	20.00

	Ivory	Decorated
Cup	4.50	15.00
5 Plate, 6¼", sherbet	2.50	8.00
1 Plate, 9¾", dinner	4.00	20.00
Plate, 11½", sandwich or cake	7.50	30.00
Saucer	1.00	6.00
2 Sherbet, low footed	7.00	25.00
Sugar, open	5.00	20.00

CHRISTMAS CANDY
Indiana Glass Company, 1950s
crystal, teal

	Crystal	Teal		Crystal	Teal
Bowl, 5¾", fruit	4.50	——	Plate, 6", bread & butter	3.00	11.00
Bowl, 7⅜", soup	7.00	55.00	1 Plate, 8¼", luncheon	5.00	25.00
Bowl, 9½", vegetable	——	650.00	Plate, 9⅝", dinner	10.00	45.00
3 Creamer	6.00	30.00	2 Plate, 11¼", sandwich	16.00	60.00
4 Cup	3.00	24.00	5 Saucer	1.00	10.00
Mayonnaise	15.00	——	6 Sugar	6.00	30.00

CIRCLE
Hocking Glass Company, 1930s
green, pink, crystal

	Green or Pink
Bowl, 4½"	20.00
Bowl, 5", flared	35.00
Bowl, 8"	35.00
Bowl, 9⅜"	40.00
Creamer	7.00
4 Cup	6.00
Goblet, 4½", wine	15.00
2 Goblet, 8 oz., water	11.00
Pitcher, 60 oz.	75.00
Pitcher, 80 oz.	40.00
Plate, 6", sherbet	2.00

	Green or Pink
Plate, 8¼", luncheon	6.00
Plate, 10", sandwich	14.00
1 Saucer with cup ring	2.50
Sherbet, 3⅛"	5.00
Sherbet, 4¾"	7.00
5 Sugar	7.00
3 Tumbler, 4 oz., juice	9.00
Tumbler, 8 oz., water	10.00
Tumbler, 10 oz.	20.00
Tumbler, 15 oz.	30.00

CLOVERLEAF
Hazel Atlas Glass Company, 1930 – 1936
crystal, pink, green, yellow, black

	Green	Yellow
Ashtray, 4", match holder in center (black only)	55.00	——
Ashtray, 5¾", match holder in center (black only)	80.00	——
Bowl, 4", dessert	50.00	40.00
Bowl, 5", cereal	58.00	60.00
Bowl, 7", salad	100.00	100.00
Bowl, 8"	125.00	——
Candy dish & cover	85.00	135.00
Creamer, footed, 3⅝"	15.00	22.00
Cup	9.00	10.00

	Green	Yellow
5 Plate, 6", sherbet	15.00	10.00
1 Plate, 8", luncheon	10.00	14.00
Plate, 10¼", grill	30.00	30.00
Salt & pepper, pr.	40.00	135.00
Saucer	3.00	4.00
Sherbet, 3" footed	12.00	14.00
Sugar, footed, 3⅝"	12.00	20.00
Tumbler, 3¾", 9 oz., flat	70.00	——
3 Tumbler, 4", 10 oz., flat, flared top	60.00	——
2 Tumbler, 5¾", 10 oz., footed	30.00	40.00

COIN GLASS
Line #1372, Fostoria Glass Company, 1958 – 1982
amber, blue, crystal, green, olive, red

	Blue	Crystal
Ashtray, 5", #1372/123	25.00	15.00
Ashtray, 7½", center coin, #1372/119	———	20.00
Ashtray, 7½", round, #1372/114	40.00	20.00
Ashtray, 10", #1372/124	50.00	22.00
Ashtray, oblong, #1372/115	20.00	10.00
Ashtray/cover, 3", #1372/110	25.00	25.00
Bowl, 8", round, #1372/179	50.00	25.00
Bowl, 8½", footed, #1372/199	90.00	45.00
Bowl, 8½", footed with cover, #1372/212	175.00	85.00
* Bowl, 9", oval, #1372/189	48.00	30.00
* Bowl, wedding with cover, #1372/162	90.00	55.00
Candle holder, 4½", pr., #1372/316	55.00	40.00
Candle holder, 8", pr., #1372/326	———	50.00
Candy box with cover, 4⅛", #1372/354	60.00	30.00
* Candy jar with cover, 6⁵⁄₁₆", #1372/347	50.00	25.00
* Cigarette box with cover, 5¾" x 4½", #1372/374	80.00	40.00
Cigarette holder with ashtray cover, #1372/372	75.00	40.00

* Items recently remade

Continued

		Blue	Crystal
	Cigarette urn, 3⅜", footed, #1372/381	45.00	20.00
	Condiment set, 4-pc. (tray, 2 shakers, and cruet), #1372/737	325.00	140.00
	Condiment tray, 9⅝", #1372/738	75.00	40.00
4	*Creamer, #1372/680	16.00	10.00
	*Cruet, 7 oz. with stopper, #1372/531	165.00	55.00
1	*Decanter with stopper, pint, 10³⁄₁₆", #1372/400	265.00	100.00
	*Jelly, #1372/448	25.00	15.00
	Lamp chimney, coach or patio, #1372/461	60.00	40.00
	Lamp chimney, hndl., courting, #1372/292	65.00	——
	Lamp, 9¾", hndl., courting, oil, #1372/310	190.00	——
	Lamp, 10⅛", hndl., courting, electric, #1372/311	200.00	——
	Lamp, 13½", coach, electric, #1372/321	250.00	95.00
3	Lamp, 13½", coach, oil, #1372/320	250.00	95.00
	Lamp, 16⅝", patio, electric, #1372/466	295.00	140.00
	Lamp, 16⅝", patio, oil, #1372/459	295.00	140.00
	Nappy, 4½", #1372/495	——	25.00
	*Nappy, 5⅜", with hndl. #1372/499	28.00	15.00
2	Pitcher, 32 oz., 6⁵⁄₁₆", #1372/453	145.00	45.00
	Plate, 8", #1372/550	——	20.00
	Punch bowl base, #1372/602	——	150.00
	Punch bowl, 14", 1½ gal., #1372/600	——	150.00
	Punch cup, #1372/615	——	30.00
	*Salver, footed, 6½" tall, #1372/630	225.00	125.00
	Shaker, 3¼", pr. with chrome top, #1372/652	65.00	25.00
	Stem, 4", 5 oz. wine, #1372/26	——	33.00
	Stem, 5¼", 9 oz., sherbet, #1372/7	——	25.00
	Stem, 10½ oz., goblet, #1372/2	——	35.00
5	*Sugar with cover, #1372/673	45.00	25.00
	Tumbler, 3⅝", 9 oz., juice/old fashioned, #1372/81	——	22.00
	Tumbler, 4¼", 9 oz., water, scotch & soda, #1372/73	——	22.00
	Tumbler, 5⅛", 12 oz., iced tea/high ball, #1372/64	——	28.00
	Tumbler, 5⅜", 10 oz., double old fashioned, #1372/23	——	28.00
	Tumbler, 5³⁄₁₆", 14 oz., iced tea, #1372/58	——	28.00
	*Urn, 12¾", footed, with cover, #1372/829	140.00	75.00
	Vase, 8", bud, #1372/799	40.00	20.00
	Vase, 10", footed, #1372/818	——	45.00

* Items recently remade

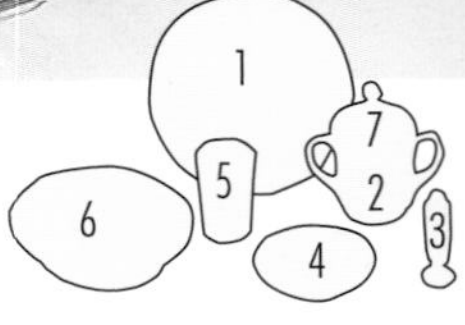

COLONIAL, "KNIFE AND FORK"
Hocking Glass Company, 1934 – 1938
pink, green, crystal

	Pink	Green
Bowl, 3¾"	65.00	—
4 Bowl, 4½", berry	20.00	14.00
Bowl, 5½", cereal	65.00	100.00
Bowl, 4½", cream soup	75.00	85.00
Bowl, 7", low soup	75.00	78.00
Bowl, 9", lg. berry	30.00	32.00
6 Bowl, 10", oval vegetable	40.00	40.00
Butter dish & cover	750.00	60.00
Creamer, 5", 16 oz. (milk pitcher)	70.00	28.00
Cup	10.00	14.00
Goblet, 3¾", 1 oz., cordial	—	30.00
Goblet, 4", 3 oz., cocktail	—	24.00
Goblet, 4½", 2½ oz., wine	—	24.00
Goblet, 5¼", 4 oz., claret	—	24.00
Goblet, 5¾", 8½ oz., water	—	30.00
Mug, 4½", 12 oz.	600.00	800.00
Pitcher, 7", 54 oz., ice lip or none	50.00	55.00
Pitcher, 7¾", 68 oz., ice lip or none	70.00	80.00
Plate, 6", sherbet	7.00	8.00

	Pink	Green
Plate, 8½", luncheon	10.00	12.00
1 Plate, 10", dinner	60.00	65.00
Plate, 10", grill	25.00	35.00
Platter, 12", oval	35.00	25.00
3 Salt & pepper, pr.	150.00	130.00
Saucer (same as sherbet plate)	7.00	8.00
Sherbet	12.00	15.00
Spoon holder or celery	135.00	130.00
2 Sugar, 5"	25.00	18.00
7 Sugar cover	65.00	27.00
Tumbler, 3", 5 oz., juice	22.00	25.00
5 Tumbler, 4", 9 oz., water	20.00	22.00
Tumbler, 11 oz	35.00	42.00
Tumbler, 12 oz., iced tea	52.00	52.00
Tumbler, 15 oz., lemonade	65.00	75.00
Tumbler, 3¼", 3 oz., footed	20.00	25.00
Tumbler, 4", 5 oz., footed	40.00	45.00
Tumbler, 5¼", 10 oz., footed	50.00	50.00
Whiskey, 2½", 1½ oz	16.00	16.00

"COLONIAL BLOCK," MODERNISTIC
Hazel Atlas Glass Company, late 1920s – early 1930s
green, pink, crystal, white

	Green or Pink		Green or Pink
Bowl, 4"	11.00	Goblet	15.00
Bowl, 7"	22.00	3 Pitcher	50.00
Butter dish	40.00	5 Sherbet	7.00
Butter tub	45.00	1 Sugar	10.00
2 Candy dish & cover, 8½"	42.00	1 Sugar cover	15.00
4 Creamer	12.00	Tumbler, 5¼", 5 oz., footed	55.00

COLONIAL FLUTED, "ROPE"
Federal Glass Company, 1928 – 1933
green, crystal

	Green
Bowl, 4", berry	15.00
Bowl, 6", cereal	18.00
Bowl, 6½", deep salad	38.00
Bowl, 7½", lg. berry	28.00
2 Creamer	10.00
Cup	9.00

	Green
Plate, 6", sherbet	4.00
1 Plate, 8", luncheon	9.00
Saucer	2.00
4 Sherbet	8.00
3 Sugar	8.00
3 Sugar cover	20.00

Not Colonial Fluted but Federal 9" used as dinner plate.

COLUMBIA
Federal Glass Company, 1938 – 1942
crystal, pink

	Crystal	Pink
Bowl, 5", cereal	17.00	——
Bowl, 8", low soup	20.00	——
Bowl, 8½", salad	20.00	——
Bowl, 10½", ruffled edge	22.00	——
4 Butter dish & cover	18.00	——
5 Cup	8.00	25.00
1 Plate, 6", bread & butter	4.00	15.00

	Crystal	Pink
2 Plate, 9½", luncheon	10.00	35.00
Plate, 11", chop	18.00	——
Saucer	2.00	10.00
6 Snack plate	20.00	——
3 Tumbler, 4 oz	25.00	——
Tumbler, 9 oz	30.00	——

CONSTELLATION, PATTERN #300
Indiana Glass Company, circa 1940
Sunset Constellation, Tiara Home Products, 1980s
crystal, amber, amberina, yellow mist, red, green

	Crystal	Colors
Basket, 11", lg. centerpiece	30.00	25.00
Basket, sm. centerpiece	20.00	—
Bowl, 6", nut, cupped	10.00	—
Bowl, jumbo salad	25.00	—
Bowl, 11", 2 hndl., oval	20.00	—
Bowl, 11½", flat rim, footed console, belled	25.00	20.00
Bowl, nappy, 3-toe	12.50	—
Bowl, punch, flat	35.00	—
Cake stand	50.00	—
Cake, sq. pedestal, footed	50.00	—
Candle, triangle, pr.	18.00	22.00
Candy with lid, 5½", 3-toe	22.50	18.00
Celery, oval, compote, low centerpiece	25.00	—
Cookie jar and lid, 9"	30.00	30.00
Creamer	10.00	—

	Crystal	Colors
Mayonnaise bowl, flat, with ladle	25.00	—
Mug	12.00	—
3 Pickle, oval, 2 hndl.	15.00	—
Pitcher, 7½"	40.00	60.00
Plate, dessert	5.00	—
1 Plate, lunch	7.50	—
Plate, mayonnaise liner	5.00	—
Plate, salad	10.00	—
Plate, 13½", serving/cake	22.00	25.00
Plate, 18", buffet	32.00	—
Platter, oval	22.50	—
Relish, 6", 3-part	15.00	—
2 Stem, 6¼", 8 oz., water	12.50	15.00
Sugar	10.00	—
4 Tumbler, flat, 2 oz.	5.00	—
Tumbler, flat, 8 oz.	12.50	—

CORONATION, "BANDED FINE RIB," "SAXON"

Hocking Glass Company, 1936 – 1940
pink, crystal, green, Royal Ruby

	Pink	Royal Ruby
3 Bowl, 4¼", berry	65.00	——
6 Bowl, 4½", 2 hdld	8.00	8.00
2 Bowl, 6½", nappy, 2 hdld	8.00	18.00
7 Bowl, 8", lg. berry, 2 hdld	16.00	18.00
4 Cup	5.00	6.50
Pitcher, 7¾", 68 oz.	695.00	——

	Pink	Royal Ruby
Plate, 6", sherbet	3.00	——
1 Plate, 8½", luncheon	5.00	——
5 Saucer	2.00	——
Sherbet	10.00	——
Tumbler, 5", 10 oz., footed	31.00	——

CREMAX
MacBeth-Evans Division of Corning Glass Works
late 1930s – early 1940s
cremax, decal decorations

	Ivory	Ivory Decorated		Ivory	Ivory Decorated
Bowl, 5¾", cereal	4.00	12.00	Plate, 6¼", bread & butter	2.00	4.00
Bowl, 9", vegetable	12.00	18.00	1 Plate, 9¾", dinner	4.00	12.00
Creamer	4.00	10.00	Plate, 11½", sandwich	5.00	20.00
2 Cup	4.00	6.00	Saucer	1.00	3.50
Cup, demitasse	11.00	———	Saucer, demitasse	4.00	———
3 Cup, egg, 6¼"	10.00	———	Sugar, open	4.00	10.00

42

CROCHETED CRYSTAL
Imperial Glass Company, 1943 – early 1950s

	Crystal
Basket, 6"	30.00
Basket, 9"	50.00
Basket, 12"	85.00
Bowl, 7", Narcissus	40.00
Bowl, 10½", salad	30.00
Bowl, 11", console	30.00
Bowl, 12", console	35.00
Buffet set, 14", plate, footed, sauce bowl, ladle	50.00
Cake stand, 12", footed	40.00
Candleholder, 4½", 2-lite	14.00
Candleholder (Narcissus bowl shape)	45.00
Celery, 10", oval	25.00
Cheese & cracker, 12", plate, footed dish	40.00
Creamer, footed	20.00
Epergne, 11", footed bowl, center vase	130.00
Hors d'oeuvre dish, 10½", 4-part, round	30.00
Lamp, 11", hurricane with shade	75.00
Mayonnaise bowl, 5¼"	12.50
Mayonnaise ladle	5.00

	Crystal
Mayonnaise plate, 7½"	7.50
Plate, 8", salad	7.50
Plate, 9½"	12.50
Plate, 13", salad bowl liner	25.00
2 Plate, 14"	30.00
Plate, 17"	40.00
1 Punch bowl, 14"	65.00
Punch cup, closed-hndl.	3.00
3 Punch cup, open-hndl.	8.00
Relish, 11½", 3-part	25.00
Stem, 4½", 3½ oz., cocktail	28.00
Stem, 5½", 4½ oz., wine	32.00
Stem, 5", 6 oz., sherbet	20.00
Stem, 7⅛", 9 oz., water goblet	30.00
Sugar, footed	20.00
Tumbler, 6", 6 oz., footed fruit juice	25.00
Tumbler, 7⅛", 12 oz., footed iced tea	30.00
Vase, 8"	35.00

"CROW'S FOOT"
Line #412 & Line #890, Paden City Glass Company, 1930s
Ritz blue, Ruby red, amber, amethyst, black, pink, crystal, white, and yellow

	Red	Other Colors
Bowl, 4⅞", sq.	25.00	12.50
Bowl, 8¾", sq.	50.00	25.00
Bowl, 6"	40.00	15.00
Bowl, 6½", round, 2½" high, 3½"base.	45.00	22.50
Bowl, 8½", sq., 2 hndl.	50.00	27.50
Bowl, 10", footed	75.00	32.50
Bowl, 10", sq, 2 hndl.	75.00	32.50
5 Bowl, 11", oval	35.00	20.00
Bowl, 11", sq.	60.00	30.00
Bowl, 11", sq., rolled edge	65.00	32.50
Bowl, 11½", 3-footed, round console..	85.00	42.50
Bowl, 11½", console	75.00	37.50
2 Bowl, cream soup, footed, flat	20.00	10.00
Bowl, nasturtium, 3-footed	185.00	95.00
Bowl, whipped cream, 3-footed	55.00	27.50
Cake plate, sq., low pedestal	85.00	42.50
Candle, round base, tall	75.00	37.50
Candle, sq., mushroom	37.50	20.00
Candlestick, 5¾"	25.00	12.50
Candy with cover, 6½", 3-part, 2 styles ..	85.00	40.00
Candy, 3-footed, round, 6⅛"wide, 3¼" high	150.00	70.00
Cheese stand, 5"	25.00	12.50
Comport, 3¼" tall, 6¼" wide	35.00	15.00
Comport ¾" tall, 7⅜" wide	50.00	35.00
Comport, 6⅝" tall, 7" wide	60.00	30.00
Creamer, flat	14.00	8.00

	Red	Other Colors
Creamer, footed	14.00	8.00
3 Cup, footed or flat	12.00	8.00
Gravy boat, flat	95.00	50.00
Gravy boat, pedestal	135.00	60.00
Mayonnaise, 3-footed	55.00	30.00
Plate, 5¾"	6.00	2.00
Plate, 8", round	12.00	4.50
1 Plate, 8½", sq.	13.00	3.50
Plate, 9¼", round, sm. dinner	30.00	12.00
Plate, 9½", round, 2 hndl.	65.00	32.50
Plate, 10⅜", round, 2 hndl.	50.00	25.00
Plate, 10⅜", sq., 2 hndl.	40.00	20.00
Plate, 10½", dinner	90.00	30.00
Plate, 11", cracker	45.00	22.50
Platter, 12"	35.00	15.00
Relish, 11", 3-part	95.00	45.00
Sandwich server, round, center-hndl...	65.00	32.50
Sandwich server, sq., center-hndl.	45.00	17.50
Saucer, 6", round	3.50	1.00
4 Saucer, 6", sq.	4.00	1.50
Sugar, flat	12.00	5.50
Sugar, footed	12.00	5.50
Tumbler, 4¼"	75.00	37.50
Vase, 4⅝" tall, 4⅛" wide	75.00	40.00
Vase, 10¼", cupped	110.00	45.00
Vase, 10¼", flared	100.00	32.50
Vase, 11¾", flared	175.00	70.00

CUBE, "CUBIST"
Jeannette Glass Company, 1929 – 1933
pink, green, crystal

	Pink	Green
Bowl, 4½", dessert	13.00	13.00
Bowl, 4½" deep	9.00	——
Bowl, 6½", salad	14.00	15.00
6 Butter dish & cover	70.00	65.00
3 Candy jar & cover, 6½"	30.00	30.00
Coaster, 3¼"	7.50	10.00
Creamer, 2⅝"	3.00	——
1 Creamer, 3³⁄₁₆"	12.00	14.00
Cup	6.00	8.00
Pitcher, 8¾", 45 oz.	235.00	255.00

	Pink	Green
Plate, 6" sherbet	3.00	3.00
Plate, 8", luncheon	7.00	9.00
2 Powder jar & cover, 3 legs	30.00	33.00
Salt & pepper, pr.	33.00	38.00
Saucer	2.50	2.50
5 Sherbet, footed	8.00	9.00
Sugar, 2⅜"	3.00	——
4 Sugar, 3"	7.00	8.00
7 Sugar/candy cover	15.00	15.00
Tumbler, 4", 9 oz.	78.00	85.00

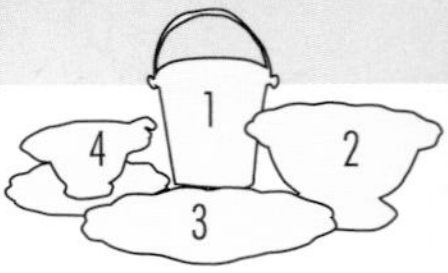

"CUPID"
Paden City Glass Company, 1930s
amber, blue, black, pink, green

	Green/Pink
2 Bowl, 8½", oval, footed	250.00
Bowl, 9¼", footed, fruit	265.00
Bowl, 9¼", center hndl.	250.00
Bowl, 10¼", fruit	215.00
Bowl, 10½", rolled edge	185.00
Bowl, 11", console	185.00
Cake plate, 11¾"	200.00
3 Cake stand, 2" high, footed	200.00
Candlestick, 5" wide, pr.	200.00
Candy with lid, footed, 5¼" high	365.00
Candy with lid, 3-part	275.00
Casserole, covered	895.00
Comport, 6¼"	195.00
Creamer, 4½", footed	135.00
Creamer, 5", footed	135.00

	Green/Pink
Cup	250.00
1 Ice bucket, 6"	295.00
Ice tub, 4¾"	295.00
4 Mayonnaise, 6" diameter, fits on 8" plate, spoon, 3-pc.	165.00
Plate, 10½"	125.00
Samovar	1,000.00
Saucer	50.00
Sugar, 4¼", footed	135.00
Sugar, 5", footed	135.00
Tray, 10¾", center hndl.	200.00
Tray, 10⅞", oval, footed	225.00
Vase, 8¼", elliptical	695.00
Vase, fan-shaped	525.00
Vase, 10"	295.00

"DAISY," NUMBER 620

Indiana Glass Company
crystal, 1933; amber, 1940; dark green and milk glass, 1960s

	Crystal	Amber		Crystal	Amber
Bowl, 4½", berry	4.50	9.00	1 Plate, 9⅜", dinner	5.00	7.00
Bowl, 4½", cream soup	4.50	10.00	Plate, 10⅜", grill	5.50	10.00
Bowl, 6", cereal	10.00	25.00	Plate, 11½", cake or sandwich	9.00	14.00
Bowl, 7⅜", berry	7.50	16.00	Platter, 10¾"	7.50	15.00
Bowl, 9⅜", deep berry	13.00	28.00	Relish dish, 3-part, 8⅜"	13.00	22.00
Bowl, 10", oval vegetable	10.00	15.00	Saucer	1.00	1.00
Creamer, footed	6.00	8.00	Sherbet, footed	5.00	8.00
Cup	3.00	4.00	2 Sugar, footed	6.00	8.00
Plate, 6", sherbet	2.00	3.00	Tumbler, 9 oz., footed	8.00	15.00
Plate, 7⅜", salad	3.50	7.00	Tumbler, 12 oz., footed	15.00	32.00
Plate, 8⅜", luncheon	3.00	5.00			

DELLA ROBBIA, #1058

Westmoreland Glass Company,
Late 1920s – 1940s

crystal decorated, opaque blue, white

	Crystal w/Trim
Basket, 9"	210.00
Basket, 12"	300.00
Bowl, 4½", nappy	30.00
Bowl, 5", finger	35.00
3 Bowl, 6", nappy, bell	35.00
Bowl, 6½", 1 hndl., nappy	35.00
Bowl, 7½", nappy	45.00
Bowl, 8", nappy, bell	65.00
Bowl, 8", bell, hndl.	85.00
Bowl, 8", heart, hndl.	135.00
Bowl, 9", nappy	115.00
Bowl, 12", footed	150.00
Bowl, 13", rolled edge	150.00
Bowl, 14", oval, flange	250.00
Bowl, 14", punch	335.00
Bowl, 15", bell	225.00
Candle, 4"	33.00
Candle, 4", 2-lite	135.00
Candy jar with cover, scalloped edge	125.00
Candy, round, flat, chocolate	110.00
4 Comport, 6½", 3⅝" high, mint, footed	40.00
Comport, 8", sweetmeat, bell	110.00
Comport, 12", footed, bell	130.00
Comport, 13", flanged	135.00
Creamer, footed	23.00
Cup, coffee	20.00
Cup, punch	15.00

	Crystal w/Trim
Pitcher, 32 oz.	260.00
Plate, 6", finger liner	10.00
2 Plate, 6⅛", bread & butter	12.00
Plate, 7¼", salad	22.00
Plate, 9", luncheon	40.00
1 Plate, 10½", dinner	150.00
Plate, 14", torte	110.00
Plate, 18"	235.00
Plate, 18", upturned edge, punch bowl liner	210.00
Platter, 14", oval	205.00
Punch bowl set, 15-pc.	995.00
Salt & pepper, pr.	80.00
Salver, 14", footed, cake	150.00
Saucer	10.00
Stem, 3 oz., wine	30.00
Stem, 3¼ oz., cocktail	25.00
Stem, 5 oz., 4¾", sherbet, high foot	22.00
Stem, 5 oz., sherbet, low foot	20.00
Stem, 6 oz., champagne	25.00
Stem, 8 oz., 6", water	32.00
Sugar, footed	22.00
Tumbler, 5 oz., ginger ale	25.00
Tumbler, 8 oz., footed	28.00
Tumbler, 8 oz., water	22.00
Tumbler 11 oz., iced tea, footed	35.00
Tumbler 12 oz., iced tea, bell, w/or w/out foot	40.00
Tumbler 12 oz., 5³⁄₁₆", iced tea, straight	42.00

DEWDROP
Jeannette Glass Company, 1953 – 1956
crystal, iridescent

	Crystal
Bowl, 4¾"	5.00
Bowl, 8½"	17.50
Bowl, 10⅜"	20.00
Butter, with cover	25.00
Candy dish, with cover, 7", round	22.00
Creamer	8.00
Cup, punch or snack	3.00
Pitcher, ½ gallon, ftd	22.00
Pitcher, flat	50.00

	Crystal
Plate, 11½"	17.50
5 Plate, snack, with indent for cup	4.00
Punch bowl base	10.00
1 Punch bowl, 6 qt.	30.00
3 Relish, leaf shape with hndl.	6.00
6 Sugar, with cover	13.00
Tray, 13", Lazy Susan with inserts	40.00
Tumbler, 9 oz., water	22.00
Tumbler, 15 oz., iced tea	33.00

DIAMOND POINT
Indiana Glass Company, circa 1966
crystal, crystal with ruby stain, crystal with gold, blue satin, green satin, black, yellow, teal, blue, amber, electric blue, carnival, milk

	Crystal with Ruby Stain
Ashtray, 5½"	5.00
Bowl, 3-toe, crimped	8.00
Bowl, 6", flat rim	5.00
6 Bowl, 6", scalloped rim	6.00
Bowl, 9¾", straight side	12.50
Bowl, 11½", low foot, scalloped	15.00
Bowl, 13½", low foot, flared	18.00
Cake stand, 10"	20.00
Candle, footed	7.50
7 Candlelamp	10.00
Candy, 4¾", with lid	10.00
Candy, 15½" tall, "chalice" with lid	25.00
Compote, 7¼" tall, flat rim	12.50
Compote, 7¼" tall, crimped rim	12.50

	Crystal with Ruby Stain
Compote, covered candy	18.00
Creamer, footed	4.00
Duet server, stand with 6" bowls	14.00
1 Stem, water	6.00
Ice tub, 11⅝", with lid (looks like cookie jar)	18.00
2 Mug	8.00
3 Pitcher	20.00
Plate, 14½", serving	15.00
Shaker	5.00
5 Sherbet, footed	4.00
Sugar, footed	4.00
4 Tumbler, 9 oz., water	4.00
Tumbler, 15 oz., tea	5.00
Vase, footed	12.00

DIAMOND QUILTED, "FLAT DIAMOND"
Imperial Glass Company, late 1920s – early 1930s
pink, blue, green, crystal, black

	Green	Blue		Green	Blue
Bowl, 4¾", cream soup	15.00	25.00	Pitcher, 64 oz.	55.00	—
Bowl, 5", cereal	10.00	15.00	1 Plate, 6", sherbet	4.00	8.00
Bowl, 5½", 1 hndl.	9.00	22.00	Plate, 7", salad	6.00	11.00
Bowl, 7", crimped edge	15.00	25.00	2 Plate, 8", luncheon	10.00	15.00
Bowl, rolled edge console	20.00	60.00	Plate, 14", sandwich	15.00	—
Cake salver, tall, 10" diameter	95.00	—	Punch bowl & stand	600.00	—
5 Candlesticks (2 styles), pr.	25.00	40.00	Sandwich server, center hndl.	25.00	50.00
4 Candy jar & cover, footed	75.00	—	Saucer	5.00	6.00
Compote & cover, 11½"	95.00	—	3 Sherbet	10.00	16.00
Creamer	12.00	15.00	Sugar	12.00	15.00
Cup	9.50	17.50	Tumbler, 9 oz., water	9.00	—
Goblet, 1 oz., cordial	12.00	—	Tumbler, 12 oz., iced tea	9.00	—
Goblet, 2 oz., wine	12.00	—	Tumbler, 6 oz., footed	8.50	—
Goblet, 3 oz., wine	12.00	—	Tumbler, 9 oz., footed	15.00	—
Goblet, 6", 9 oz., champagne	11.00	—	Tumbler, 12 oz., footed	20.00	—
Ice bucket	55.00	85.00	Whiskey, 1½ oz.	10.00	—
Mayonnaise set: ladle, plate, 3-footed dish	40.00	60.00			

DIANA
Federal Glass Company, 1937 – 1941
pink, amber, crystal

	Pink	Amber
Ashtray, 3½"	3.50	——
Bowl, 5", cereal	8.00	14.00
Bowl, 5½", cream soup	30.00	20.00
2 Bowl, 9", salad	22.00	18.00
1 Bowl, 11", console fruit	40.00	15.00
Bowl, 12", scalloped edge	50.00	20.00
Candy jar & cover, round	53.00	50.00
Coaster, 3½"	8.00	10.00
Creamer, oval	16.00	9.00
6 Cup	18.00	9.00
Cup, demitasse, 2 oz. & 4½" saucer set	35.00	——

	Pink	Amber
4 Plate, 6", bread & butter	4.00	2.00
Plate, 9½", dinner	16.00	9.00
Plate, 11¾", sandwich	25.00	12.50
Platter, 12", oval	33.00	15.00
Salt & pepper, pr.	95.00	100.00
7 Saucer	5.00	2.00
3 Sherbet	10.00	12.00
Sugar, open, oval	16.00	8.00
5 Tumbler, 4⅛", 9 oz.	55.00	30.00

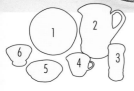

DOGWOOD, "APPLE BLOSSOM," "WILD ROSÉ"
MacBeth Evans Company, 1929 – 1932
pink, green, crystal, yellow

	Pink	Green
5 Bowl, 5½", cereal	25.00	35.00
Bowl, 8½", berry	55.00	125.00
Bowl, 10¼", fruit	625.00	295.00
Cake plate, 11", heavy solid foot	1,250.00	—
Cake plate, 13", heavy solid foot	150.00	145.00
Coaster, 3¼"	650.00	—
4 Creamer, 2½", thin	16.00	35.00
Creamer, 3¼", thick	20.00	—
Cup, thin or thick	15.00	32.00
2 Pitcher, 8", 80 oz., decorated	200.00	575.00
Pitcher, 8", 80 oz. (American Sweetheart style)	650.00	—
Plate, 6", bread & butter	9.00	10.00
Plate, 8", luncheon	8.00	10.00

	Pink	Green
Plate, 9¼", dinner	28.00	—
Plate, 10½", grill AOP or border design only	23.00	28.00
Plate, 12", salver	32.00	—
Platter, 12", oval (rare)	695.00	—
Saucer	4.00	8.00
6 Sherbet, low footed	28.00	125.00
Sugar, 2½", thin	16.00	40.00
Sugar, 3¼", thick	15.00	—
Tumbler, 3½", 5 oz., decorated	195.00	—
Tumbler, 4", 10 oz., decorated	45.00	100.00
3 Tumbler, 4¾", 11 oz., decorated	45.00	105.00
Tumbler, 5", 12 oz., decorated	75.00	125.00
Tumbler, moulded band	22.00	—

DORIC
Jeannette Glass Company, 1935 – 1938
pink, green, Delphite, yellow

		Pink	Green
	Bowl, 4½", berry	13.00	14.00
	Bowl, 5", 2 hndl. cream soup	—	595.00
	Bowl, 5½", cereal	80.00	95.00
	Bowl, 8¼", large berry	33.00	38.00
	Bowl, 9", 2 hndl.	30.00	42.00
	Bowl, 9", oval vegetable	42.00	50.00
6	Butter dish & cover	80.00	100.00
	Cake plate, 10", 3 legs	25.00	30.00
	Candy dish & cover, 8"	40.00	45.00
	Candy dish, 3-part	12.00	12.00
	Coaster, 3"	18.00	20.00
	Creamer, 4"	17.00	15.00
4	Cup	11.00	14.00
	Pitcher, 6", 36 oz., flat	50.00	55.00
1	Pitcher, 7½", 48 oz., footed	750.00	1,350.00
	Plate, 6", sherbet	6.00	7.00

		Pink	Green
	Plate, 7", salad	25.00	25.00
	Plate, 9", dinner	20.00	20.00
2	Plate, 9", grill	25.00	25.00
	Platter, 12", oval	33.00	35.00
	Relish tray, 4" x 4"	16.00	14.00
	Relish tray, 4" x 8"	25.00	20.00
7	Salt & pepper, pr.	33.00	37.50
5	Saucer	4.00	5.00
	Sherbet, footed	12.00	15.00
	Sugar	15.00	15.00
	Sugar cover	20.00	30.00
	Tray, 10", hndl.	28.00	30.00
	Tray, 8" x 8", serving	40.00	40.00
	Tumbler, 4½", 9 oz., flat	75.00	115.00
3	Tumbler, 4", 10 oz., footed	85.00	100.00
	Tumbler, 5", 12 oz., footed	95.00	140.00

DORIC AND PANSY
Jeannette Glass Company, 1937 – 1938
pink, crystal, ultramarine

	Pink	Ultra-marine		Pink	Ultra-marine
4 Bowl, 4½", berry	15.00	20.00	Sugar, open	——	85.00
Bowl, 8", lg. berry	30.00	100.00	Tray, 10", hndl.	——	38.00
Bowl, 9", hndl.	25.00	45.00	3 Tumbler, 4½", 9 oz.	——	90.00
Butter dish & cover	——	350.00			
6 Cup	——	18.00	**"PRETTY POLLY PARTY DISHES"**		
Creamer	——	85.00	Cup	30.00	40.00
Plate, 6", sherbet	6.00	10.00	Saucer	5.00	5.00
Plate, 7", salad	——	45.00	Plate	6.00	10.00
1 Plate, 9", dinner	——	40.00	Creamer	30.00	40.00
2 Salt & pepper, pr.	——	350.00	Sugar	30.00	40.00
5 Saucer	——	5.00	14-pc. set	230.00	300.00

55

EARLY AMERICAN PRESCUT

Anchor Hocking Glass Corp.,
1960 – 1999

crystal, amber, blue green, red, and black, some with painted designs

	Crystal
Ashtray, 4", #700/690	5.00
Ashtray, 5"	10.00
Ashtray, 7¾", #718-G	12.00
Bowl, 4¼", #726, smooth rim	15.00
Bowl, 5¼", #775, scalloped rim	7.00
Bowl, 6¾", 3-toed, #768	4.00
Bowl, 7¼", scalloped rim	18.00
Bowl, 7¼", round, #767	6.00
Bowl, 8¾" #787	10.00
Bowl, 9", console, #797	15.00
Bowl, 9", oval, #776	7.00
Bowl, 9⅜", gondola dish, #752	4.00
Bowl, 10¾", salad, #788	12.00
Bowl, 11¾", paneled, #794	150.00
Bowl, dessert, 5⅜", #765	2.50
Butter, bottom with metal handle and knife	15.00
Butter with cover, ¼ lb., #705	6.00
Cake plate, 13½", footed, #706	28.00
Candlestick, 7" x 5⅝", double, #784	22.50
Candy with lid, 5¼", #744	10.00
Candy with cover, 7¼" x 5½", #792	12.00
Chip & dip, 10¾"; bowl, 5¼", brass finish holder, #700/733	25.00
Coaster, #700/702	2.00
Cocktail shaker, 9", 30 oz.	795.00
Creamer, #754	3.00
Cruet, with stopper, 7¾", #711	6.00
Cup, punch or snack, 6 oz. (no star)	2.00
Lazy Susan, 9-pc., #700/713	40.00

	Crystal
Oil lamp	210.00
Pitcher, 18 oz., #744	8.00
Pitcher, 40 oz., sq.	40.00
Pitcher, 60 oz., #791	15.00
Plate, 6¾", no ring, salad with indent	35.00
Plate, 6¾", with ring, for 6 oz. cup	40.00
Plate, 11", 4-part with swirl dividers	125.00
Plate, 11"	12.00
Plate, 11¾", deviled egg/relish, #750	30.00
Plate, 13½", serving, #790	12.50
Punch set, 15-pc.	33.00
Relish, 8½", oval, 2-part, #778	5.00
Relish, 10", divided, tab hndl., #770	7.00
Relish, 13½", 5-part	22.00
Server, 12 oz., syrup, #707	18.00
Shakers, pr., metal tops, #700/699	5.00
Shakers, pr., plastic tops, #725	5.00
Shakers, pr., 2¼", individual, #700/736	35.00
Sherbet, 3½", 6 oz., footed	495.00
Sugar, with lid, #753	4.00
Tray, 6½" x 12", hostess, #750	12.50
Tray, creamer/sugar, #700/671	3.00
Tumbler, 5 oz., 4", juice, #730	4.00
Tumbler, 10 oz., 4½", #731	3.00
Tumbler, 15 oz., 6", iced tea, #732	20.00
Vase, 5", footed, bud	795.00
Vase, 6" x 4½", basket/block, #704/205	18.00
Vase, 8½", #741	8.00
Vase, 10", #742	12.50

EMERALD GLO
Paden City and Fenton Art Glass Company, 1940s – 1950s
emerald green

	Emerald Green
Candleholders, pr., ball with metal cups	40.00
Casserole with metal cover	45.00
Cheese dish with metal top and hndl.	85.00
Cocktail shaker, 10", 26 oz.	65.00
Condiment set (2 jars, metal lids, spoons, and tray)	65.00
Condiment set (3 jars, metal lids, spoons, and tray)	95.00
Creamer	20.00
1 Creamer/sugar, individual, with metal lid, on metal tray	50.00
3 Creamer/sugar, individual (metal), with marmalade on metal tray	55.00
Cruet	25.00
2 Ice bucket, metal holder, and tongs	75.00
Marmalade with metal lid and spoon	28.00
Mayonnaise, divided, with metal underliner and glass spoons	40.00

	Emerald Green
Oil bottle	25.00
Relish, 9", divided, with metal hndl.	35.00
Relish, 9", tab hndl., with metal hndl.	40.00
Relish, heart-shaped	35.00
Salad bowl with metal base, fork, and spoon	75.00
Salad bowl, 10"	33.00
Server, 5-part, with metal covered center	65.00
4 Shaker	20.00
Sugar	20.00
Sugar with metal lid and liner	25.00
5 Syrup with metal lid and liner	45.00
Tidbit, 2-tier (bowls 6" and 8")	50.00
Tray, 8½", hndl.	35.00
Tumbler, 2⅝", 1 oz.	10.00

ENGLISH HOBNAIL
Westmoreland Glass Company, 1920s – 1970s
crystal, pink, amber, turquoise, cobalt, green

	Pink or Green
Ashtray, several shapes	20.00
Bowls, 4½", 5" sq. & round	25.00
Bowl, cream soup	25.00
Bowls, 6", several styles	18.00
Bowls, 8", several styles	45.00
Bowls, 8", footed & 2 hndl.	85.00
Bowls, 11" & 12", nappies	55.00
Bowls, relish, oval, 8" & 9"	30.00
Bowl, relish, oval, 12"	40.00
Candlesticks, 3½", pr.	50.00
Candlesticks, 8½", pr.	80.00
1 Candy dish, ½ lb., cone-shaped	55.00
Candy dish & cover, 3 feet	70.00
Celery dish, 9"	35.00
Celery dish, 12"	40.00
Cigarette box	40.00
5 Cologne bottle	40.00
Creamer, footed or flat	24.00
Cup	18.00
Decanter, 20 oz. with stopper	125.00
Demitasse cup & saucer	70.00
Egg cup	36.00
Goblet, 2 oz., wine	30.00

	Pink or Green
Goblet, 3 oz., cocktail	20.00
Goblet, 6¼", 8 oz.	30.00
Grapefruit, ½", flange rim	20.00
Lamp, 6¼", electric	75.00
Lamp, 9¼"	125.00
Marmalade & cover	40.00
Pitcher, 23 oz.	150.00
Pitcher, 38 oz.	225.00
Pitcher, 60 oz.	295.00
2 Pitcher, ½ gallon, straight sides	300.00
Plate, 5½" & 6½", sherbet	9.00
Plate, 7¼", pie	9.00
Plate, 8", round or sq.	13.00
Plate, 10", dinner	45.00
4 Salt & pepper, pr., round or sq. base	65.00
Salt dip, 2" footed & with place card holder	20.00
Saucer	4.00
Sherbet	14.00
3 Sugar, footed or flat	24.00
Tumbler, 3¾", 5 oz. or 8 oz	24.00
Tumbler, 4", 10 oz., iced tea	28.00
Tumbler, 5", 12 oz., iced tea	32.00

FANCY COLONIAL #582
Imperial Glass Co.., circa 1914
crystal, pink, green, teal, some iridized Rubigold and Ice (rainbow washed crystal)

	All Colors*
Bonbon, 5½", hndl.	25.00
Bottle, water, no stopper	75.00
Bowl, 3½", nappy	12.00
Bowl, 4½", nappy	15.00
Bowl, 4½", rim-foot berry	15.00
Bowl, 5", nappy or olive	16.00
Bowl, 5", footed, 2 hndl.	22.00
4 Bowl, 5", nut or lily (cupped rim)	22.00
Bowl, 5", rim-foot berry	20.00
5 Bowl, 6", nappy	20.00
Bowl, 7", nappy or rim-foot berry	35.00
Bowl, 7", lily	40.00
Bowl, 8", 2 hndl. berry	65.00
Bowl, 8", nappy or salad	38.00
Bowl, 8", spoon tray (hump edge)	38.00
Bowl, 8", lily (cupped)	45.00
Bowl, 8", rim-foot berry	38.00
Bowl, 9", rim-foot berry	40.00
Butter and cover	80.00
Celery, 12", oval	50.00
Comport, 4", footed	25.00
Comport, 5½", footed	30.00
1 Comport, 6¼", footed	35.00
2 Creamer, footed	25.00
Cup, custard, flare edge	17.50
Cup, punch, straight edge	12.00
Goblet, egg cup, low foot deep	30.00
Goblet, low foot, café parfait	25.00
Mayonnaise with liner, flat	50.00
Oil bottle with stopper, 6¼ oz.	65.00
Oil bottle, 5½ oz., bulbous, with stopper	75.00
Pickle, 8", oval	30.00
Pitcher, 3 pint	125.00
Plate, 5¾"	12.00

	All Colors*
Plate, 7½", salad	20.00
Plate, 10½", cake	45.00
Plate, mayonnaise liner	12.00
Salt & pepper, pair	75.00
Salt, table, or footed almond, hndl.	18.00
Saucer	8.00
Sherbet, 3¼", low foot, flare rim or not	22.50
Sherbet, 4¼", low foot	22.50
Sherbet, 4¾", footed jelly	25.00
Spoon (flat open sugar)	20.00
Stem, 1 oz., cordial, deep	30.00
Stem, 2 oz., wine, deep	25.00
Stem, 3 oz., cocktail, shallow	18.00
Stem, 3 oz., port, deep	20.00
Stem, 4½ oz., cocktail, shallow	16.00
Stem, 4 oz., burgundy, deep	25.00
Stem, 5 oz. claret, deep	30.00
Stem, 6 oz., champagne, deep	18.00
Stem, 6 oz., saucer/champagne, shallow	18.00
Stem, 8 oz., goblet, deep	20.00
Stem, 10 oz., goblet, deep	22.00
Sugar with lid, flat	30.00
3 Sugar, ftd., hotel, open	25.00
Tumbler, 2 oz., whiskey	20.00
Tumbler, 4 oz.	15.00
Tumbler, 5 oz., belled rim or not	15.00
Tumbler, 6 oz.	15.00
Tumbler, 8 oz.	18.00
Tumbler, 10 oz.	18.00
Tumbler, 12 oz., iced tea	20.00
Tumbler, 14 oz., iced tea	22.00
Vase, 8", low foot, flare	65.00
Vase, 10", flat, bead base, ruffled rim	85.00
Vase, 12", flat, bead base, ruffled rim	110.00

*Crystal subtract 25%; teal add 30%.

FIRE-KING DINNERWARE "ALICE"
Anchor Hocking Company, 1940s
Jade-ite, Vitrock, Vitrock with trims

	Jade-ite	Vitrock		Jade-ite	Vitrock
2 Cup	7.00	5.00	3 Saucer	3.00	2.00
1 Plate	26.00	14.00			

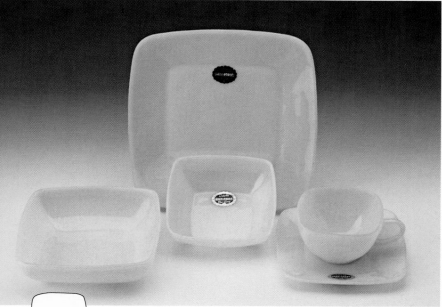

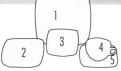

FIRE-KING DINNERWARE "CHARM"
Anchor Hocking Glass Corporation, 1940s – 1960s
Jade-ite, white/trim, Azur-ite, Forest Green, Royal Ruby

	Azur-ite	Jade-ite
3 Bowl, 4¾", dessert	6.00	18.00
2 Bowl, 6", soup	15.00	35.00
Bowl, 7⅜", salad	18.00	60.00
Creamer	12.00	20.00
4 Cup	4.00	12.00
Plate, 6⅝", salad	9.00	35.00

	Azur-ite	Jade-ite
1 Plate, 8⅜", luncheon	9.00	22.00
Plate, 9¼", dinner	18.00	30.00
Platter	25.00	60.00
5 Saucer	1.50	5.00
Sugar	12.00	20.00

FIRE-KING DINNERWARE FLEURETTE
Anchor Hocking Glass Corporation, 1958 – 1960

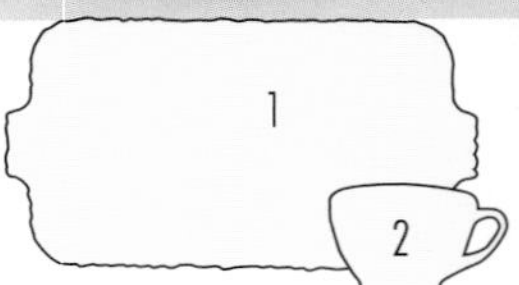

	Fleurette
Bowl, 4⅝", dessert	3.00
Bowl, 5", chili	22.00
Bowl, 6⅝", soup plate	12.00
Bowl, 8¼", vegetable	11.00
Creamer	5.00
2 Cup, 5 oz., snack	3.00
Cup, 8 oz.	4.00
Mug	85.00
Plate, 6¼", bread & butter	10.00

	Fleurette
Plate, 7⅜", salad	10.00
Plate, 9⅛", dinner	5.00
Platter, 9" x 12"	14.00
Saucer, 5¾"	1.00
Sugar	5.00
Sugar cover	5.00
1 Tray, 11"x 6", snack	4.00
Tumbler, 9½ oz., water	125.00

FIRE-KING DINNERWARE "GAME BIRDS"
Anchor Hocking Glass Corporation, 1959 – 1962
white with decals

	White w/decals
Ashtray, 5¼"	15.00
Bowl, 4⅝", dessert	5.00
Bowl, 5", soup or cereal	8.00
Bowl, 8¼", vegetable	65.00
Creamer	22.00
Mug, 8 oz.	8.00
Plate, 6¼", bread & butter	8.00

	White w/decals
1 Plate, 9⅛", dinner	6.50
Platter, 12" x 9"	65.00
Sugar	22.00
Sugar cover	5.00
Tumbler, 5 oz., juice	32.00
4 Tumbler, 11 oz., iced tea	10.00

FIRE-KING DINNERWARE GRAY LAUREL
Anchor Hocking Glass Corporation, 1952 – 1963

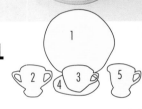

	Gray Laurel
Bowl, 4⅞", dessert	7.00
Bowl, 7⅝", soup plate	12.00
Bowl, 8¼", vegetable	18.00
5 Creamer, footed	5.00
3 Cup, 8 oz.	4.00

	Gray Laurel
Plate, 7⅜", salad	8.00
1 Plate, 9⅛", dinner	10.00
Plate, 11", serving	16.00
4 Saucer, 5¾"	3.00
2 Sugar, footed	5.00

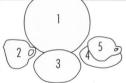

FIRE-KING DINNERWARE HONEYSUCKLE
Anchor Hocking Glass Corporation, 1958 – 1960
white with decals

	White w/decals			White w/decals
Bowl, 4⅝", dessert	4.00	1	Plate, 9⅛", dinner	6.00
Bowl, 6⅝", soup plate	9.00		Platter, 9" x 12"	16.00
Bowl, 8¼", vegetable	16.00	4	Saucer, 5¾"	1.50
2 Creamer	5.00		Sugar	5.00
5 Cup, 8 oz.	4.00		Sugar cover	5.00
Mug	50.00		Tumbler, 5 oz., juice	20.00
3 Plate, 6¼", bread & butter	10.00		Tumbler, 9 oz., water	15.00
Plate, 7⅜", salad	5.00		Tumbler, 16 oz., iced tea	18.00

FIRE-KING DINNERWARE "JANE RAY"
Anchor Hocking Company, 1945 – 1960s
Jade-ite, Vitrock, white

	Jade-ite
5 Bowl, 4⅞", dessert	10.00
Bowl, 5⅞", oatmeal	16.00
Bowl, 7⅝", soup	18.00
Bowl, 8¼", vegetable	22.00
7 Cup	6.00
Cup, demitasse	30.00
4 Creamer	10.00

	Jade-ite
Plate, 7¾", salad	10.00
2 Plate, 9⅛", dinner	10.00
1 Platter, 12"	18.00
8 Saucer	1.00
Saucer, demitasse	35.00
3 Sugar	8.00
3 Sugar cover	18.00

FIRE-KING DINNERWARE PEACH LUSTRE
Anchor Hocking Glass Corporation, 1952 – 1963

	Peach Lustre
3 Bowl, 4⅞", dessert	4.00
Bowl, 7⅝", soup plate	10.00
1 Bowl, 8¼", vegetable	10.00
6 Creamer, footed	4.00
4 Cup, 8 oz.	3.50

	Peach Lustre
Plate, 7⅜", salad	9.00
2 Plate, 9⅛", dinner	5.00
Plate, 11", serving	14.00
5 Saucer, 5¾"	1.00
7 Sugar, footed	4.00

FIRE-KING DINNERWARE "PHILBE"

Anchor Hocking Glass Company, 1937 – 1938
blue, pink, green, and crystal

	Pink or Green
Bowl, 5½", cereal	45.00
Bowl, 7¼", salad	80.00
Bowl, 10", oval vegetable	90.00
Candy jar, 4", low with cover	725.00
Cookie jar with cover	950.00
Creamer, 3¼", footed	150.00
Cup	110.00
Goblet, 7¼", thin, 9 oz.	225.00
Pitcher, 6", juice, 36 oz.	625.00
Pitcher, 8½", 54 oz.	925.00
Plate, 6", sherbet	65.00
2 Plate, 8", luncheon	37.50

	Pink or Green
Plate, 10", heavy sandwich	75.00
Plate, 10½", salver	75.00
4 Plate, 10½", grill	75.00
1 Plate, 11⅝", salver	65.00
Platter, 12", closed hndl.	125.00
Saucer, 6" (same as sherbet plate)	65.00
5 Sugar, 3¼", footed	135.00
Tumbler, 3½", footed juice	150.00
Tumbler, 4", 9 oz., flat water	105.00
Tumbler, 5¼", footed, 10 oz.	80.00
Tumbler, 6½", footed, 15 oz. iced tea	85.00

FIRE-KING DINNERWARE & OVEN WARE PRIMROSE
Anchor Hocking Glass Corporation, 1960 – 1962
white with decal

	White w/decal
3 Bowl, 4⅝", dessert	3.50
Bowl, 6⅝", soup plate	9.00
Bowl, 8¼", vegetable	14.00
Cake pan, 8", round	12.00
Cake pan, 8", sq.	12.00
Casserole, pt., knob cover	9.00
Casserole, 1½ qt., oval, au gratin cover	15.00
Casserole, 1 qt., knob cover	12.00
Casserole, 1½ qt., knob cover	12.00
Casserole, 2 qt., knob cover	16.00
Creamer	5.00
Cup, 5 oz., snack	3.00
4 Cup, 8 oz.	3.00
2 Custard, 6 oz., low or dessert	3.50

	White w/decal
Pan, 5" x 9", baking, with cover	18.00
Pan, 5" x 9", deep loaf	14.00
Pan, 6½" x 10½", utility baking	12.00
Pan, 8" x 12½", utility baking	35.00
6 Plate, 7⅜", salad	5.00
1 Plate, 9⅛", dinner	7.00
Platter, 9" x 12"	15.00
5 Saucer, 5¾"	1.00
Sugar	5.00
Sugar cover	5.00
Tray, 11" x 6", rectangular, snack	5.00
Tumbler, 5 oz., juice (white)	30.00
Tumbler, 10 oz., iced tea (crystal)	50.00
Tumbler, 11 oz., water (white)	25.00

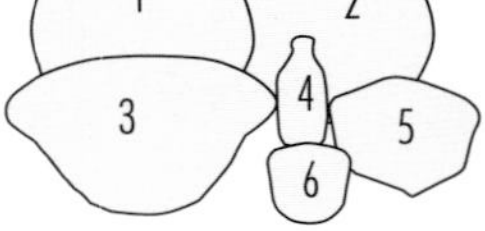

FIRE-KING OVEN GLASS
Anchor Hocking Glass Company
blue, 1940s; crystal, 1950s

	Blue
Baker, 1 pt., round or sq.	8.00
Baker, 1 qt.	12.00
Baker, 1½ qt.	16.00
Baker, 2 qt.	16.00
Cake pan (no tabs), 8¾"	45.00
Casserole, 1 pt., knob hndl. cover	14.00
Casserole, 1 qt., knob hndl. cover	18.00
Casserole, 1½ qt., knob hndl. cover	22.00
Casserole, 2 qt., knob hndl. cover	22.00
Casserole, 1 qt., pie plate cover	18.00
Casserole, 1½qt., pie plate cover	20.00
Casserole, 2 qt., pie plate cover	25.00
Casserole, 10 oz., tab hndl. cover	13.00
Coffee mug, 7 oz.	25.00
Cup, 8 oz., measuring	20.00
Custard cup, 5 oz.	5.00
6 Custard cup, 6 oz., 2 styles	5.00
Loaf pan, 9⅛" deep	20.00
4 Nurser, 4 oz.	20.00

	Blue
Nurser, 8 oz.	30.00
Pie plate, 4⅜", individual	20.00
Pie plate, 5⅜", deep dish	20.00
2 Pie plate, 8⅜"	9.00
Pie plate, 9"	10.00
1 Pie plate, 9⅝"	10.00
Pie plate, 10⅜", juice saver	120.00
Percolator top, 2⅛"	5.00
5 Refrigerator jar & cover, 4½" x 5"	15.00
Refrigerator jar & cover, 5⅛" x 9⅛"	30.00
Roaster, 8¾	55.00
Roaster, 10⅜"	75.00
Table server, tab hndl. (hot plate)	20.00
Utility bowl, 6⅞"	18.00
Utility bowl, 8⅜"	20.00
3 Utility bowl, 10⅛"	22.00
Utility pan, 10½" x 2" deep	25.00
Utility pan, 8⅛" x 12½"	100.00

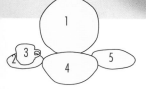

FIRE-KING OVEN WARE BLUE MOSAIC
Anchor Hocking Glass Corporation, 1962 – late 1960s

Bowl, 4⅝", dessert	8.00
Bowl, 6⅝", soup plate	15.00
4 Bowl, 8¼", vegetable	20.00
Creamer	8.00
3 Cup, 7½ oz.	4.00
5 Plate, 7⅜", salad	8.00

1 Plate, 10", dinner	9.00
Platter, 9" x 12"	18.00
2 Saucer, 5¾"	2.00
Sugar	8.00
Sugar cover	5.00
Tray, 10" x 7½", oval, snack	6.00

FIRE-KING OVEN WARE TURQUOISE BLUE
Anchor Hocking Glass Corporation, 1950s

	Blue
	Blue
6 Ashtray, 3½"	10.00
7 Ashtray, 4⅝"	12.00
8 Ashtray, 5¾"	14.00
Batter bowl, with spout	375.00
Bowl, 4½", berry	10.00
Bowl, 5", cereal	15.00
Bowl, 6⅝", soup/salad	25.00
Bowl, 8", vegetable	25.00
Bowl, tear, mixing, 1 pt.	33.00
2 Bowl, tear, mixing, 1 qt.	33.00
3 Bowl, tear, mixing, 2 qt.	38.00
4 Bowl, tear, mixing, 3 qt.	63.00
Bowl, round, mixing, 1 qt.	23.00

	Blue
	Blue
Bowl, round, mixing, 2 qt.	28.00
Bowl, round, mixing, 3 qt.	30.00
Creamer	8.00
5 Cup	5.00
1 Mug, 8 oz.	25.00
Plate, 6⅛"	24.00
Plate, 7¼"	12.00
Plate, 9"	14.00
Plate, 9", with cup indent	6.00
Plate, 10"	33.00
Relish, 3-part	13.00
Saucer	1.50
Sugar	8.00

FIRE-KING OVEN WARE "SHELL"
Anchor Hocking Glass Corporation, 1960s – 1975
Jade-ite, lustre, white

	Jade-ite "Shell"	Lustre "Shell"		Jade-ite "Shell"	Lustre "Shell"
3 Bowl, 4¾", dessert	14.00	4.00	Plate, 7¼", salad	18.00	3.50
4 Bowl, 6⅜", cereal	25.00	10.00	1 Plate, 10", dinner	25.00	7.00
Bowl, 7⅝", soup plate	32.00	15.00	2 Platter, 9½" x 13"	48.00	———
5 Bowl, 8½", vegetable	28.00	18.00	6 Saucer, 5¾"	4.00	2.00
Creamer, footed	25.00	10.00	Saucer, 4¾", demitasse	———	10.00
7 Cup, 8 oz.	10.00	5.00	8 Sugar, footed	25.00	10.00
Cup, 3¼ oz., demitasse	———	10.00	8 Sugar cover	45.00	8.00

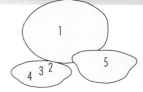

FIRE-KING OVEN WARE SUNRISE
Anchor Hocking Glass Corporation, circa 1953

2 Bowl, 4⅞", fruit or dessert	5.00
3 Bowl, 6⅜", cereal	18.00
4 Bowl, 7⅝", soup plate	18.00
5 Bowl, 8¼", vegetable	22.00
Creamer, flat	10.00
Cup, 8 oz.	6.50
Plate, 7⅜", salad	8.00
Plate, 9⅛", dinner	10.00
1 Platter, 12" x 9"	18.00
Saucer, 5¾"	3.00
Sugar lid, for flat sugar	10.00
Sugar, flat, tab hndl.	10.00

FIRE-KING OVEN WARE WHEAT
Anchor Hocking Glass Corporation, 1962 – late 1960s

	Blue
Bowl, 4⅝", dessert	3.50
Bowl, 5", chili	25.00
Bowl, 6⅝", soup plate	8.00
Bowl, 8¼", vegetable	12.00
Cake pan, 8", round	11.00
Cake pan, 8", sq.	10.00
Casserole, 1 pt., knob cover	8.00
Casserole, 1 qt., knob cover	10.00
Casserole, 1½ qt., knob cover	11.00
Casserole, 1½ qt., oval, au gratin cover	14.00
Casserole, 2 qt., knob cover	15.00
Creamer	5.00
Cup, 5 oz., snack	3.00
Cup, 8 oz.	4.00

	Blue
2 Custard, 6 oz., low or dessert	3.00
Mug	30.00
Pan, 5" x 9", baking, with cover	16.00
Pan, 5" x 9", deep loaf	12.00
Pan, 6½" x 10½" x 1½", utility baking	12.00
Pan, 8" x 12½" x 2", utility baking	18.00
Plate, 7⅜", salad	8.00
1 Plate, 10", dinner	6.00
Platter, 9" x 12"	15.00
3 Saucer, 5¾"	1.00
Sugar	4.50
Sugar cover	5.00
Tray, 11" x 6", rectangular, snack	4.00

FLORAGOLD, "LOUISA"
Jeannette Glass Company, 1950s
iridescent, Shell Pink, crystal

		Iridescent
3	Bowl, 4½", sq.	5.00
	Bowl, 5½", cereal, round	42.00
	Bowl, 5½", ruffled fruit	7.00
	Bowl, 8½", sq.	14.00
	Bowl, 9½", salad, deep	42.00
	Bowl, 9½", ruffled	8.00
	Bowl, 12", ruffled, lg. fruit	7.00
	Butter dish & cover, ¼ lb., oblong	25.00
2	Butter dish & cover, round	45.00
	Candlesticks, double branch, pr.	50.00
	Candy or cheese dish & cover, 6¾"	50.00
	Candy, 5¼" long, 4 feet	8.00
	Coaster/ashtray, 4"	6.00
	Creamer	9.00
	Cup	6.00

		Iridescent
1	Pitcher, 64 oz.	35.00
	Plate, 5¾", sherbet	8.00
	Plate, 8½", dinner	35.00
	Plate or tray, 13½"	25.00
	indent on 13½" plate	65.00
	Platter, 11¼"	25.00
	Salt & pepper, plastic tops	50.00
	Saucer (same as sherbet plate)	8.00
	Sherbet, low footed	14.00
	Sugar	6.50
	Sugar lid	12.00
	Tumbler, 10 oz., footed	18.00
4	Tumbler, 11 oz., footed	18.00
	Tumbler, 15 oz., footed	100.00
	Vase or celery	495.00

FLORAL, "POINSETTIA"
Jeannette Glass Company, 1931 – 1935
pink, green, delphite
See Reproduction Section, Page 202

	Pink	Green
Bowl, 4", berry	20.00	22.00
Bowl, 5½", cream soup	750.00	750.00
Bowl, 7½", salad	30.00	30.00
Bowl, 8", covered vegetable	55.00	70.00
Bowl, 9", oval vegetable	22.00	28.00
Butter dish & cover	105.00	105.00
Candlesticks, 4", pr.	100.00	100.00
Candy jar & cover	40.00	45.00
Coaster, 3¼"	12.00	12.00
Compote, 9"	1,000.00	1,025.00
Creamer, flat	14.00	16.00
Cup	10.00	10.00
Ice tub, 3½" high, oval	950.00	995.00
Lamp	325.00	325.00
Pitcher, 5½", 23 or 24 oz., flat	——	495.00
Pitcher, 8", 32 oz., footed cone	40.00	42.00
Pitcher, 10¼", 48 oz., lemonade	295.00	295.00
Plate, 6", sherbet	5.00	6.00
Plate, 8", salad	12.00	13.00
Plate, 9", dinner	17.00	20.00

	Pink	Green
Plate, 9", grill	——	300.00
Platter, 10¾", oval	20.00	23.00
Refrigerator dish & cover, 5", sq.	——	75.00
Relish dish, oval, 2-part	20.00	22.00
Salt & pepper, 4", footed, pr. (beware reproductions)	45.00	50.00
Salt & pepper, 6", flat	55.00	——
Saucer	7.00	7.00
Sherbet	16.00	18.00
Sugar	10.00	12.00
Sugar/candy cover	16.00	18.00
Tray, 6", sq., closed hndl.	22.00	25.00
Tumbler, 4", 5 oz., footed juice	20.00	23.00
Tumbler, 4¾", 7 oz., footed water	18.00	20.00
1 Tumbler, 5¼", 9 oz., footed lemonade	55.00	60.00
Vase, 3-legged rose bowl	——	525.00
Vase, 3-legged, flared (also in crystal)	——	495.00
Vase, 6⅞" tall (8-sided)	——	425.00

FLORAL AND DIAMOND BAND

U.S. Glass Company, 1927 – 1931

crystal, pink, green

	Pink	Green		Pink	Gree
Bowl, 4½", berry	10.00	12.00	Plate, 8", luncheon	38.00	40.0
Bowl, 5¾", nappy, hndl.	15.00	15.00	4 Sherbet	6.00	7.0
Bowl, 8", lg. berry	20.00	20.00	Sugar, sm.	10.00	12.0
1 Butter dish & cover	125.00	115.00	Sugar, 5¼"	15.00	15.0
Compote, 5½" tall	20.00	25.00	Sugar lid	55.00	65.0
Creamer, sm.	10.00	12.00	3 Tumbler, 4", water	20.00	20.0
Creamer, 4¾"	18.00	20.00	Tumbler, 5", iced tea	35.00	40.0
2 Pitcher, 8", 42 oz.	110.00	115.00			

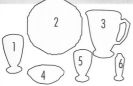

FLORENTINE NO. 1, "POPPY NO. 1"
Hazel Atlas Glass Company, 1934 – 1936
pink, green, crystal, yellow, cobalt
See Reproduction Section, Page 202

	Green	Yellow
Ashtray, 5½"	20.00	28.00
Bowl, 5", berry	12.00	18.00
Bowl, 6", cereal	25.00	30.00
Bowl, 8½", lg. berry	30.00	35.00
Bowl, 9½", oval vegetable & cover	65.00	85.00
Butter dish & cover	125.00	180.00
Coaster/ashtray, 3¾"	20.00	22.00
Creamer	11.00	22.00
Creamer, ruffled	45.00	——
Cup	9.00	13.00
Pitcher, 6½", 36 oz., footed	40.00	55.00
Pitcher, 7½", 54 oz., flat ice lip or none	75.00	135.00
Plate, 6", sherbet	6.00	7.00

* Beware reproductions.

	Green	Yellow
Plate, 8½", salad	10.00	14.00
2 Plate, 10", dinner	22.00	24.00
Plate, 10", grill	14.00	20.00
Platter, 11½", oval	25.00	28.00
6 *Salt & pepper, footed	36.00	55.00
Saucer	3.00	4.00
Sherbet, 3 oz., footed	12.00	15.00
Sugar	9.00	12.00
Sugar cover	18.00	30.00
Sugar, ruffled	40.00	——
5 Tumbler, 3¾", 5 oz., footed juice	16.00	28.00
1 Tumbler, 4¾", 10 oz., footed water	22.00	25.00
Tumbler, 5¼", 12 oz., footed iced tea	28.00	32.00

FLORENTINE NO. 2, "POPPY NO. 2"

Hazel Atlas Glass Company, 1932 – 1935
pink, green, yellow, crystal, cobalt blue
See Reproduction Section, Page 203

	Green	Yellow
Bowl, 4½", berry	14.00	18.00
Bowl, 4¾", cream soup	17.00	20.00
Bowl, 5½"	35.00	40.00
Bowl, 6", cereal	33.00	38.00
Bowl, 8", lg. berry	30.00	40.00
Bowl, 9", oval vegetable & cover	——	85.00
Butter dish & cover	100.00	150.00
3 Candlesticks, 2¾", pr.	50.00	70.00
Candy dish & cover	90.00	150.00
Coaster, 3¼"	12.00	22.00
Coaster/ashtray, 3¾"	17.00	32.00
Coaster/ashtray, 5½"	20.00	35.00
Compote, 3½", ruffled	40.00	——
7 Creamer	9.00	12.00
5 Cup	9.00	10.00
Custard cup or gelatin	60.00	85.00
Gravy boat	——	55.00
Pitcher, 7½", 28 oz., cone footed	32.00	35.00
Pitcher, 7½", 48 oz.	75.00	135.00
Pitcher, 8", 76 oz.	115.00	450.00

	Green	Yellow
Plate, 6", sherbet	4.00	6.00
Plate, 6¼", with indent for custard	——	30.00
Plate, 8½", salad	9.00	8.00
Plate, 10", dinner	16.00	15.00
Plate, 10¼", grill	16.00	18.00
1 Platter, 11", oval	16.00	25.00
Platter, 11½" for gravy boat	——	60.00
Relish dish, 10", 3-part or plain	28.00	35.00
6 Salt & pepper, pr.	40.00	45.00
4 Saucer	3.00	4.00
Sherbet, footed	10.00	10.00
2 Sugar	10.00	11.00
2 Sugar cover	15.00	25.00
Tumbler, 3½", 5 oz., juice	14.00	22.00
Tumbler, 4", 9 oz., water	14.00	20.00
Tumbler, 5", 12 oz., iced tea	38.00	55.00
Tumbler, 3¼", 5 oz., footed	16.00	18.00
Tumbler, 4", 5 oz., footed	15.00	16.00
Tumbler, 4½", 9 oz., footed	32.00	32.00
Vase or parfait, 6"	30.00	55.00

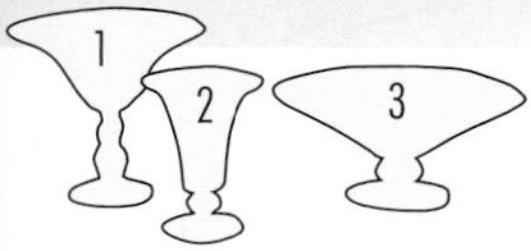

FLOWER GARDEN WITH BUTTERFLIES, "BUTTERFLIES AND ROSES"

U.S. Glass Company, late 1920s

pink, green, blue-green, canary yellow, amber, black

	Pink or Green		Pink or Green
Ashtray, matchbook holders	175.00	Plate, 10"	42.50
Candlesticks, 4", pr.	55.00	Powder jar, footed	145.00
Candlesticks, 8", pr.	135.00	Powder jar, flat	75.00
Candy dish & cover, 7½"	130.00	Sandwich server, center handle	65.00
Candy dish, open, 6"	40.00	Saucer	25.00
Cheese & cracker set, 4" compote, 10" plate	80.00	Sugar, open	70.00
Cologne bottle, 7½" tall, footed	225.00	Tray, 5½" x 10", oval	60.00
3 Comport, 4¾" x 10¼"	65.00	Tray, rectangular, 11¾" x 7¾"	75.00
1 Comport, 7¼" x 8¼"	80.00	2 Vase, 6¼"	100.00
Console bowl, 10", footed	85.00	Vase, 8" black	210.00
Creamer	70.00	Vase, 10½"	135.00
Cup	70.00		
Plate, 8", 2 styles	16.00		

"FLUTE & CANE," "SUNBURST & CANE," "CANE," "HUCKABEE"

Semi-Colonial No. 666 and 666Z, Imperial Glass Co., circa 1921
crystal, pink, green, Rubigold, Caramel slag

	Crystal*
Bowl, 4½", fruit	10.00
Bowl, 6½", oval, pickle	16.00
Bowl, 6½", sq.	15.00
2 Bowl, 7½", salad	25.00
4 Bowl, 7½", ruffled	28.00
Bowl, 8½", lg. fruit	30.00
Bowl, crème soup, 5½"	20.00
Butter with lid, sm. powder box look	35.00
Butter, dome lid	55.00
6 Celery, 8½", oval, 2 hndl.	22.00
Celery, tall, 2 hndl.	40.00
Compote, 6½", oval, footed, 2 hndl.	30.00
3 Compote, 6½", ruffled top	25.00
Compote, 7½", stem with bowl	25.00
Compote, 7½", stem, flat	25.00
Creamer	15.00
Cup, custard	12.00

*Add 50% for colors.

	Crystal*
Molasses, nickel top	70.00
Oil bottle with stopper, 6 oz.	45.00
Pitcher, 22 oz., 5¼"	45.00
Pitcher, 51 oz.	65.00
Pitcher, tall/slender	75.00
Plate, 6"	15.00
Salt & pepper	45.00
5 Sherbet, 3½", stem	12.00
Spooner open sm. sugar	15.00
Stem, 1 oz., cordial	25.00
Stem, 3 oz., wine	18.00
Stem, 6 oz., champagne	15.00
Stem, 9 oz., water	18.00
1 Sugar with lid	20.00
Tumbler, 9 oz.	25.00
Vase, 6"	35.00

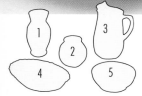

FOREST GREEN
Anchor Hocking, 1950s – 1967
dark green glass

	Green
Ashtray	5.00
Bowl, 4¾", dessert	7.00
5 Bowl, 5¾", round	7.00
Bowl, 6", soup, sq.	14.00
Bowl, 7⅜", salad, sq.	14.00
4 Bowl, 8½", oval	22.00
Bowl, 9", oval	20.00
Creamer, flat	6.00
Cup	5.00
Plate, 6⅝", salad, sq.	5.00
Plate, 8⅜", luncheon, sq.	7.00
Plate, 9¼", dinner, sq.	22.00

	Green
3 Pitcher, 24 oz.,	18.00
Pitcher, 3 qt., round	30.00
Platter, rectangular	20.00
Saucer	1.50
Sherbert	5.00
Sugar, flat	6.00
Tumbler, 5 oz.	4.00
Tumbler, 10 oz.	7.00
2 Vase, 4", ivy	4.50
1 Vase, 6⅜"	6.50
Vase, 9"	12.00

"FORTUNE"
Hocking Glass Company, 1937 – 1938
pink, crystal

	Pink
6 Bowl, 4", berry	10.00
Bowl, 4½", dessert	10.00
Bowl, 4½", hndl.	10.00
Bowl, 5¼", rolled edge	20.00
Bowl, 7¾", salad or lg. berry	28.00
5 Candy dish & cover, flat	28.00

	Pink
2 Cup	12.00
1 Plate, 6", sherbet	8.00
Plate, 8", luncheon	28.00
3 Saucer	5.00
Tumbler, 3½", juice, 5 oz.	10.00
4 Tumbler, 4", water, 9 oz.	12.00

*Double price of crystal for colors.

"FRUITS"
Hazel Atlas and Other Glass Companies, 1931 – 1953
pink, green, crystal

	Pink	Green		Pink	Green
Bowl, 5", cereal	30.00	40.00	6 Sherbet	12.00	12.00
Bowl, 8", berry	55.00	95.00	Tumbler, 3½", juice	——	80.00
4 Cup	8.00	8.00	2 Tumbler, 4" 1 fruit	18.00	20.00
3 Pitcher, 7", flat bottom	——	125.00	1 Tumbler, 4" combination of fruits	22.00	30.00
Plate, 8", luncheon	12.00	12.00	Tumbler, 5", 12 oz.	——	150.00
5 Saucer	3.00	4.00			

GEORGIAN, "LOVEBIRDS"
Federal Glass Company, 1931 – 1936
green, crystal

	Green
4 Bowl, 4½", berry	8.00
6 Bowl, 5¾", cereal	25.00
Bowl, 6½", deep	60.00
3 Bowl, 7½", lg. berry	55.00
Bowl, 9", oval vegetable	55.00
5 Butter dish & cover	80.00
Cold cuts server, 18½", wood with seven 5" openings for 5" coasters	995.00
Creamer, 3", footed	12.00
Creamer, 4", footed	18.00
Cup	10.00
Hot plate, 5" center design	80.00

	Green
2 Plate, 6", sherbet	7.00
Plate, 8", luncheon	10.00
1 Plate, 9¼", dinner	25.00
Plate, 9¼", center design only	20.00
Platter, 11½", closed hndl.	60.00
Saucer	3.00
Sherbet	11.00
Sugar, 3", footed	10.00
Sugar, 4", footed	18.00
Sugar cover, 3"	45.00
Tumbler, 4", flat, 9 oz.	60.00
Tumbler, 5¼", flat, 12 oz.	110.00

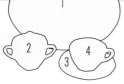

GOLDEN GLORY
Federal Glass Company, 1959 – 1966; 1978 – 1979

Bowl, 4⅞", dessert 4.00	Plate, 10", dinner... 7.00
Bowl, 6⅜", soup.. 9.00	Platter, 11¼", round.. 15.00
Bowl, 8½", vegetable...12.00	1 Platter, 12", oval... 13.00
Bowl, 8", rimmed soup 12.00	3 Saucer .... .50
Creamer... 5.00	2 Sugar 4.00
4 Cup 3.00	2 Sugar lid 5.00
Plate, 7⅜", salad... 3.00	Tumbler, 9 oz., footed... 12.00
Plate, 9⅛", dinner... 5.00	Tumbler, 10 oz., 5" 10.00

GOTHIC, "BIG TOP," "PEANUT BUTTER GLASS"

Hazel Atlas, circa 1950s
crystal, white

	Crystal
6 Cup	6.00
7 Saucer	2.00
3 Plate, 8", luncheon	7.00

*White, $5.00

	Crystal
1 Sherbet, 3⅝", 8 oz.	3.00
2 Tumbler, 5¼", 7 oz., juice	20.00
4 Tumbler, 5¾", 10 oz., tea	5.00*

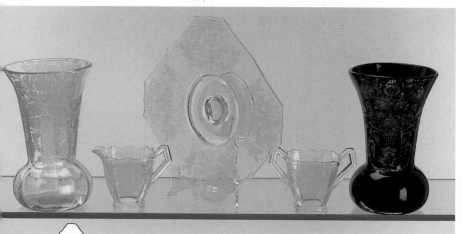

GOTHIC GARDEN
Paden City Glass Co., 1930s
pink, green, black, yellow, and crystal

	All Colors
Bowl, 9", tab hndl.	65.00
Bowl, 10", footed	85.00
Bowl, 10⅛", hndl.	95.00
Bowl, 10½", oval, hndl.	110.00
3 Cake plate, 10½", footed	90.00
Candy, flat	130.00
Comport, tall, deep top	65.00
2 Creamer	40.00
Cup	40.00

	All Colors
Plate, 6"	15.00
Plate, 11", tab hndl.	65.00
Saucer	10.00
Server, 9¾", center hndl.	65.00
4 Sugar	40.00
Vase, 6½"	130.00
1 Vase, 8"	175.00
Vase, 9½"	135.00

HARP
Jeannette Glass Company, 1954 – 1957
crystal and crystal with gold or silver rims

	Crystal		Crystal
4 Ashtray/coaster	5.00	2 Plate, 7"	12.00
Coaster	4.50	6 Saucer	10.00
5 Cup	33.00	Tray, rectangular	33.00
3 Cake stand, 9"	28.00	1 Vase, 6"	25.00

HERITAGE
Federal Glass Company, late 1930s – 1960s
crystal, pink, blue, green

	Crystal
Bowl, 5", berry	8.00
Bowl, 8½", lg. berry	30.00
Bowl, 10½", fruit	15.00
Cup	6.00
Creamer, footed	20.00

	Crystal
Plate, 8", luncheon	7.00
1 Plate, 9¼", dinner	12.00
Plate, 12", sandwich	15.00
Saucer	2.00
2 Sugar, open, footed	18.00

HEX OPTIC, "HONEYCOMB"
Jeannette Glass Company, 1928 – 1932
pink, green

	Pink or Green
6 Bowl, 4¼", berry, ruffled	10.00
5 Bowl, 7½", lg. berry, ruffled	16.00
Butter dish & cover, rectangular, 1 lb. size	100.00
Bucket reamer	70.00
7 Creamer, 2 styles of hndl.	7.00
3 Cup, 2 styles of hndl.	10.00
Ice bucket, metal hndl.	32.00
Pitcher, 5", 32 oz., sunflower motif in bottom	25.00
Pitcher, 8", flat	135.00
Pitcher, 9", 48 oz., footed	40.00
Plate, 6", sherbet	2.50
1 Plate, 8", luncheon	5.00

	Pink or Green
Platter, 11", round	15.00
Refrigerator dish, 4" x 4"	18.00
Salt & pepper, pr.	35.00
2 Saucer	2.00
4 Sugar, 2 styles of hndl.	7.00
Sugar shaker	250.00
Sherbet, 5 oz., footed	7.00
Tumbler, 3¾", 9 oz.	4.50
Tumbler, 5", 12 oz., tea	7.00
Tumbler, 5¾", footed	9.00
Tumbler, 7", footed	10.00
Whiskey, 2", 1 oz.	9.00

HOBNAIL
Hocking Glass Company, 1934 – 1936
crystal, crystal w/red trim, pink

	Crystal
Bowl, 5½", cereal	5.00
Bowl, 7", salad	5.50
Cup	4.50
Creamer, footed	9.00
Decanter & stopper, 32 oz.	35.00
Goblet, water, 10 oz.	8.00
Goblet, iced tea, 13 oz.	10.00
Pitcher, milk, 18 oz.	20.00
Pitcher, 67 oz.	25.00
Plate, 6", sherbet	1.50

	Crystal
2 Plate, 8½", luncheon	5.00
5 Saucer	1.50
Sherbet	3.00
Sugar, footed	9.00
Tumbler, juice, 5 oz.	4.00
Tumbler, water, 9 oz., 10 oz.	5.00
Tumbler, iced tea, 5¼", 15 oz.	15.00
4 Tumbler, footed wine, 3 oz.	5.00
Tumbler, footed cordial, 2 oz.	6.00
Whiskey, 1½ oz., flat	7.00

HOLIDAY, "BUTTON AND BOWS"

Jeannette Glass Company, 1947 – 1949

pink, iridescent

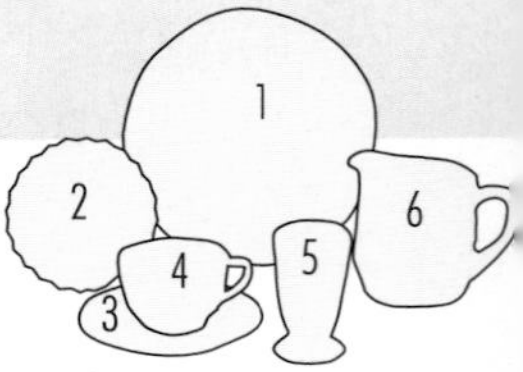

	Pink		Pin
2 Bowl, 5⅛", berry	12.50	Plate, 6", sherbet	6.0
Bowl, 7¾", soup	55.00	1 Plate, 9", dinner	18.0
Bowl, 8½", lg. berry	33.00	Plate, 13¾", chop	115.0
Bowl, 9½", oval vegetable	28.00	Platter, 11⅜", oval	24.0
Bowl, 10¾", console	140.00	Sandwich tray, 10½"	15.0
Butter dish & cover	50.00	3 Saucer, 2 styles	4.0
Cake plate, 10½", 3-legged	125.00	Sherbet	7.5
Candlesticks, 3", pr.	125.00	Sugar	10.0
Creamer, footed	12.00	Sugar cover	15.0
4 Cup, 2 sizes	8.00	Tumbler, 4", 10 oz., flat	20.0
6 Pitcher, 4¾", milk, 16 oz.	65.00	5 Tumbler, 4", footed	40.0
Pitcher, 6¾", 52 oz.	40.00	Tumbler, 6", footed	150.0

HOMESPUN, "FINE RIB"
Jeannette Glass Company, 1939 – 1940
pink, crystal

	Pink
Bowl, 4½", closed handles	18.00
Bowl, 5", cereal	32.00
Bowl, 8¼", lg. berry	32.00
Butter dish & cover	60.00
Coaster/ashtray	6.50
Creamer, footed	12.50
Cup	13.00
Plate, 6", sherbet	6.00
Plate, 9¼", dinner	20.00
Platter, 13", closed hndl.	20.00
Saucer	4.00
Sherbet, low flat	20.00
Sugar, footed	10.00
Tumbler, 3⅞", 6 oz.	22.00

	Pink
Tumbler, 4", water, 9 oz.	22.00
2 Tumbler, 5¼", iced tea, 13 oz.	33.00
Tumbler, 4", 5 oz., footed	8.00
Tumbler, 6¼", 15 oz., footed	33.00
Tumbler, 6⅜", 15 oz., footed	33.00

CHILD'S TEA SET

Cup	30.00
Saucer	10.00
Plate	10.00
Teapot	50.00
Teapot cover	90.00
Set of 14 pieces	340.00

INDIANA CUSTARD, "FLOWER AND LEAF BAND"

Indiana Glass Company

ivory or custard, early 1930s; white, 1950s

	Ivory
Bowl, 5½", berry	10.00
Bowl, 6½", cereal	25.00
Bowl, 7½", flat soup	28.00
Bowl, 9", lg. berry	25.00
Bowl, 9½", oval vegetable	25.00
2 Butter dish & cover	50.00
5 Cup	30.00
Creamer	14.00
4 Plate, 5¾", bread & butter	6.00

	Ivory
Plate, 7½", salad	12.00
Plate, 8⅞", luncheon	14.00
Plate, 9¾", dinner	20.00
1 Platter, 11½", oval	30.00
6 Saucer	4.00
Sherbet	75.00
3 Sugar	8.00
3 Sugar cover	20.00

IRIS, "IRIS AND HERRINGBONE"
Jeannette Glass Company, 1928 – 1932; 1950; 1970
crystal, iridescent
See Reproduction Section, Pages 204 – 205

	Crystal	Iridescent
Bowl, 4½", berry, beaded	35.00	7.00
Bowl, 5", sauce	10.00	22.00
Bowl, 5", cereal	100.00	——
Bowl, 7½", soup	135.00	65.00
Bowl, 8", lg. berry, beaded	75.00	22.00
Bowl, 9½", salad	15.00	10.00
Bowl, 11", fruit, ruffled	15.00	14.00
Bowl, 11", fruit, straight	55.00	——
Butter dish & cover	47.50	45.00
Candlesticks, pr.	40.00	45.00
Candy jar & cover	160.00	——
*Coaster	60.00	
Creamer, footed	12.00	12.00
Cup	14.00	14.00
Demitasse cup	35.00	150.00
Demitasse saucer	130.00	250.00
Goblet, 4", wine	——	20.00

		Crystal	Iridescent
	Goblet, 4½", wine	15.00	——
	Goblet, 5½", 4 oz.	20.00	495.00
	Goblet, 5½", 8 oz.	20.00	295.00
	Pitcher, 9½", footed	35.00	38.00
	Plate, 5½", sherbet	12.00	10.00
	Plate, 8", luncheon	85.00	——
1	*Plate, 9", dinner	35.00	40.00
	Plate, 11¾", sandwich	35.00	33.00
7	Saucer	7.00	8.00
5	Sherbet, 2½", footed	22.00	14.00
	Sherbet, 4", footed	24.00	295.00
	Sugar	11.00	11.00
	Sugar cover	14.00	12.00
	*Tumbler, 4", flat	90.00	
2	Tumbler, 6", footed	16.00	17.00
	*Tumbler, 6½", footed	20.00	——
	Vase, 9"	25.00	25.00

*Beware reproductions.

JAMESTOWN
Fostoria Glass Company, 1958 – 1982
amber, amethyst, blue, brown,
crystal, green, pink, red

	Amber	Ruby
Bowl, 4½", dessert, #2719/421	8.50	20.00
Bowl, 10", salad, #2719//211	21.00	60.00
Bowl, 10", 2 hndl. serving, #2719/648	21.00	70.00
Butter with cover, ¼ pound, #2719/300	24.00	65.00
Cake plate, 9½", hndl., #2719/306	16.00	45.00
Celery, 9¼", #2719/360	18.00	40.00
1 Cream, 3½", footed, #2719/681	11.00	25.00
Jelly with cover, 6⅛", #2719/447	32.50	80.00
Pickle, 8⅜", #2719/540	21.00	45.00
Pitcher, 7⁵⁄₁₆", 48 oz., ice jug, #2719/456	40.00	145.00
Plate, 8", #2719/550	8.50	20.00
Plate, 14", torte, #2719/567	26.00	65.00
Relish, 9⅛", 2-part, #2719/620	16.00	37.50
Salad set, 4-pc. (10" bowl, 14" plate with wood fork & spoon), #2719/286	55.00	135.00
Salver, 7" high, 10" diameter, #2719/630	60.00	150.00
2 Sauce dish with cover, 4½", #2719/635	18.00	40.00

	Amber	Ruby
3 Shaker, 3½", with chrome top, pr., #2719/653	26.00	50.00
Stem, 4⁵⁄₁₆", 4 oz., wine, #2719/26	10.00	21.00
*Stem, 4¼", 6½ oz., sherbet, #2719/7	6.50	15.00
*Stem, 4⅛", 7 oz., sherbet, #2719/7	6.50	15.00
*Stem, 5¾", 9½ oz., goblet, #2719/2	10.00	16.00
*Stem, 5⅞", 10 oz., goblet, #2719/2	10.00	16.00
4 Sugar, 3½", footed, #2719/679	11.00	25.00
Tray, 9⅜", hndl. muffin, #2719/726	26.00	65.00
Tumbler, 4¼", 9 oz., #2719/73	9.00	25.00
Tumbler, 4¾", 5 oz., juice, #2719/88	9.00	22.00
Tumbler, 5⅛", 12 oz., #2719/64	9.00	22.00
Tumbler, 6", 11 oz., footed tea, #2719/63	10.00	21.00
Tumbler, 6", 12 oz., footed tea, #2719/63	10.00	21.00

*Remade

JUBILEE
Lancaster Glass Company, Early 1930s
yellow, pink, crystal

	Pink	Yellow
Bowl, 8", 3-footed, 5⅛" high	210.00	180.00
Bowl, 9", handled fruit	——	125.00
Bowl, 11½", flat fruit	175.00	150.00
Bowl, 11½", 3-footed	225.00	195.00
Bowl, 11½", 3-footed, curved in	——	195.00
Bowl, 13", 3-footed	225.00	195.00
Candlestick, pr.	185.00	185.00
Candy jar, with lid, 3-footed	295.00	295.00
Cheese & cracker set	175.00	175.00
Creamer	30.00	16.00
3 Cup	28.00	12.00
Mayonnaise & plate	165.00	150.00
with original ladle	185.00	170.00
Plate, 7", salad	18.00	11.00
Plate, 8¾", luncheon	20.00	10.00
Plate, 13½", sandwich	60.00	45.00

	Pink	Yellow
Plate, 14", 3-footed	——	175.00
4 Saucer, 2 styles	8.00	4.00
Sherbet, 3", 8 oz.	——	65.00
Stem, 4", 1 oz., cordial	——	250.00
Stem, 4⅞", 3 oz.	——	110.00
2 Stem, 5½", 7 oz., sherbet/ champagne	——	65.00
Stem, 7½", 11 oz.	——	160.00
5 Sugar	30.00	15.00
Tray, 11", 2 hndl. cake	60.00	35.00
Tumbler, 5", 6 oz., footed juice	——	95.00
Tumbler, 6", 10 oz., water	60.00	28.00
Tumbler, 6⅛", 12½ oz., iced tea	——	135.00
Tray, 11", center-hndl. sandwich	130.00	135.00
Vase, 12"	150.00	195.00

KING'S CROWN, THUMBPRINT
Line No. 4016, U.S. Glass Tiffin Company,
Late 1800s – 1960s; Indiana Glass Company, 1970s

	Ruby Flashed
Ashtray, 5¼", sq.	35.00
4 Bowl, 4", finger	18.00
Bowl, 5", mayonnaise	50.00
Bowl, 5¾"	20.00
Bowl, 6", diameter, footed, wedding or candy	160.00
Bowl, 8¾", 2 hndl., crimped bonbon	100.00
Bowl, 9¼", salad	85.00
Bowl, 10½", footed, wedding or candy, with cover	145.00
Bowl, 11½", 4½" high, crimped	125.00
Bowl, 11¼", cone	85.00
Bowl, 12½", center edge, 3" high	120.00
Bowl, 12½", flower floater	80.00
Bowl, crimped, footed	115.00
Bowl, flared, footed	100.00
Bowl, straight edge	80.00
Cake salver, 12½", footed	75.00
Candleholder, sherbet type	22.50
Candleholder, 2-lite, 5½"	115.00
Candy box, 6", flat, with cover	65.00
Cheese stand	30.00
Compote, 7¼", 9¾" diameter	65.00
Compote, 7½", 12" diameter, footed, crimped	145.00
Compote, sm., flat	30.00
Creamer	20.00
5 Cup	8.00
Lazy Susan, 24", 8½" high, with ball bearing spinner	395.00
Mayonnaise, 3-pc. set	85.00
Pitcher	215.00

	Ruby Flashed
Plate, 5", bread & butter	8.00
Plate, 7⅜", mayonnaise liner	12.50
Plate, 7⅜", salad	12.00
1 Plate, 9¾", snack with indent	12.00
Plate, 10", dinner	38.00
Plate, 14½", torte	100.00
Plate, 24", party	175.00
Plate, 24", party server (with punch foot)	325.00
Punch bowl foot	150.00
Punch bowl, 2 styles	775.00
Punch cup	12.00
Punch set, 15-pc. with foot	1,275.00
Punch set, 15-pc. with plate	1,050.00
Relish, 14", 5-part	135.00
Saucer	5.00
Stem, 2 oz., wine	7.00
Stem, 2¼ oz., cocktail	12.50
2 Stem, 4 oz., claret	14.00
Stem, 4 oz., oyster cocktail	7.00
Stem, 5½ oz., sundae or sherbet	7.00
Stem, 9 oz., water goblet	12.00
Sugar	20.00
Tumbler, 4 oz., juice, footed	10.00
Tumbler, 4½ oz., juice	12.00
Tumbler, 8½ oz., water	10.00
3 Tumbler, 11 oz., iced tea	12.00
Tumbler, 12 oz., iced tea, footed	20.00
Vase, 9", bud	125.00
Vase, 12¼", bud	135.00

LACED EDGE, "KATY BLUE"
Imperial Glass Company, Early 1930s
blue with opalescent edge, green with opalescent edge

	Blue or Green			Blue or Green
Bowl, 4½", fruit	22.00		Plate, 6½", bread & butter	13.00
Bowl, 5"	30.00		Plate, 8", salad	25.00
3 Bowl, 5½"	30.00		Plate, 10", dinner	65.00
Bowl, 7", soup	65.00		Plate, 12", luncheon (per	
Bowl, 9", vegetable	100.00		catalog description)	75.00
1 Bowl, 11", divided oval	105.00		Platter, 13"	165.00
Bowl, 11", oval	135.00		Saucer	7.00
2 Candlestick, double, pr.	150.00		Sugar	30.00
4 Cup	28.00		Tidbit, with 8" & 10" plates	110.00
Creamer	30.00		Tumbler, 9 oz	40.00
Mayonnaise, 3-pc.	135.00			

LAKE COMO
Anchor Hocking Glass Company, 1934 – 1937
white with blue or red decoration

Bowl, 6", cereal	25.00
Bowl, flat soup	75.00
1 Bowl, vegetable, 9¾"	40.00
5 Creamer, footed	20.00
3 Cup, regular	20.00
Cup, St. Denis	24.00
Plate, salad, 7¼"	15.00
Plate, dinner, 9¼"	30.00
Platter, 11"	70.00
6 Salt & pepper, pr.	35.00
4 Saucer, regular or St. Denis	6.00
2 Sugar, footed	20.00

LARGO

Line #220, Paden City Glass Co., Late 1937 – 1951;
Canton Glass Co., 1950s
amber, crystal with ruby flash, light blue, red

	Amber/ Crystal	Blue/ Red
Ashtray, 3", rectangle	16.00	30.00
Bowl, 5"	15.00	25.00
Bowl, 6", deep	18.00	35.00
Bowl, 7½"	20.00	37.50
Bowl, 7½", crimped	22.50	45.00
Bowl, 9", tab hndl.	30.00	70.00
3 Bowl, 11⅝", 3½" deep, tri-footed, flared rim	35.00	80.00
Bowl, 12¾", 4¾" deep, tri-footed, flat rim	35.00	80.00
5 Cake plate, pedestal	35.00	95.00
Candleholder	30.00	55.00
7 Candy, flat with lid, 3-part	35.00	95.00
Cigarette box, 4" x 3½" x 1½"	30.00	65.00
6 Comport, cracker	15.00	25.00

	Amber/ Crystal	Blue/ Red
Comport, double spout, pedestal	35.00	75.00
Comport, fluted rim, pedestal	35.00	75.00
1 Comport, 6½" x 10", plain rim, pedestal	32.50	70.00
Creamer, footed	18.00	35.00
Cup	15.00	30.00
Mayonnaise, toed	22.00	55.00
4 Plate, 6⅝"	8.00	15.00
Plate, 8"	10.00	20.00
2 Plate, 10¾", cheese with indent	20.00	40.00
Sugar, footed	18.00	40.00
Saucer	5.00	10.00
Tray, 10¾", tri-footed, serving	25.00	75.00
Tray, 14", 5-part, relish	40.00	——

LAUREL
McKee Glass Company, 1930s
French ivory, jade green, white opal, and Poudre blue

	Ivory	Jade		Ivory	Jade
4 Bowl, 4¾", berry	9.00	15.00	Salt & pepper	50.00	90.00
Bowl, 6", cereal	12.00	30.00	5 Saucer	3.50	5.00
Bowl, 6", 3 legs	15.00	30.00	Sherbet	10.00	22.00
Bowl, 9", lg. berry	28.00	45.00	3 Sherbet, champagne, 5"	30.00	—
Bowl, 9¾", oval vegetable	28.00	55.00	Sugar, short	10.00	25.00
Bowl, 10½", 3 legs	40.00	60.00	Sugar, tall	14.00	25.00
Bowl, 11"	40.00	60.00	Tumbler, 4½", 9 oz., flat	30.00	75.00
Candlesticks, 4", pr.	35.00	65.00	2 Tumbler, 5", 12 oz., flat	50.00	—
Cheese dish & cover	58.00	110.00			
Creamer, short	10.00	25.00			
Creamer, tall	12.00	25.00	**CHILDREN'S LAUREL TEA SET**		
6 Cup	8.00	16.00	Creamer	25.00	90.00
Plate, 6", sherbet	10.00	16.00	Cup	22.00	45.00
Plate, 7½", salad	10.00	20.00	Plate	8.00	18.00
1 Plate, 9⅛", dinner	13.00	25.00	Saucer	6.00	10.00
Plate, 9⅛", grill	15.00	25.00	Sugar	25.00	90.00
Platter, 10¾", oval	25.00	55.00	14-pc. set	195.00	490.00

LINCOLN INN
Fenton Glass Company, Late 1920s
amethyst, cobalt, black, red, green, pink, crystal, jade, opaque, green

	Blue/Red	Other Colors		Blue/Red	Other Colors
Ashtray	17.50	12.00	Pitcher, 7¼", 46 oz.	800.00	650.00
Bonbon, hndl., sq.	15.00	12.00	Plate, 6"	9.00	4.50
Bonbon, hndl., oval	16.00	12.00	2 Plate, 8"	15.00	8.00
Bowl, 5", fruit	15.00	9.00	Plate, 9¼"	45.00	12.00
7 Bowl, 6", cereal	25.00	9.00	Plate, 12"	65.00	17.50
Bowl, 6", crimped	25.00	9.00	6 Salt & pepper, pr.	225.00	175.00
Bowl, hndl., olive	18.00	10.00	Sandwich server, center hndl.	150.00	100.00
Bowl, finger	20.00	12.50	4 Saucer	5.00	3.50
Bowl, 9¼", footed	80.00	30.00	1 Sherbet, 4¾"	22.00	12.50
Bowl, 10½", footed	80.00	35.00	Sugar	20.00	15.00
Candy dish, footed, oval	45.00	20.00	Tumbler, flat juice, 4 oz.	30.00	10.00
Comport	30.00	15.00	8 Tumbler, 5 oz., footed	32.00	11.00
Creamer	22.50	15.00	Tumbler, 9 oz., footed	30.00	14.00
5 Cup	12.00	12.00	Tumbler, 12 oz., footed	50.00	18.00
3 Goblet, water	30.00	17.50	Vase, 9¾"	165.00	85.00
Goblet, wine	32.00	17.50	Vase, 12", footed	250.00	125.00
Nut dish, footed	25.00	12.00			

LORAIN, "BASKET," "NO. 615"
Indiana Glass Company, 1929 – 1932
green, yellow, crystal

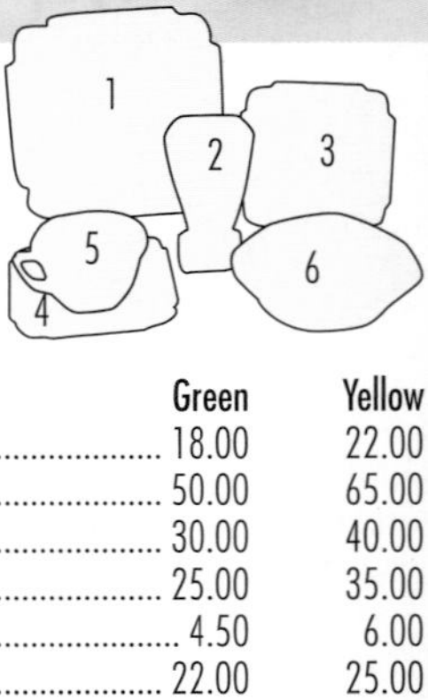

	Green	Yellow		Green	Yellow
6 Bowl, 6", cereal	50.00	85.00	Plate, 8⅜", luncheon	18.00	22.00
Bowl, 7¼", salad	60.00	85.00	1 Plate, 10¼", dinner	50.00	65.00
Bowl, 8", deep berry	125.00	175.00	Platter, 11½"	30.00	40.00
Bowl, 9¾", oval vegetable	50.00	55.00	Relish, 8", 4-part	25.00	35.00
Creamer, footed	16.00	20.00	4 Saucer	4.50	6.00
5 Cup	10.00	12.00	Sherbet, footed	22.00	25.00
Plate, 5½", sherbet	7.00	9.00	Sugar, footed	16.00	20.00
3 Plate, 7¾", salad	12.00	12.00	2 Tumbler, 4¾", 9 oz., footed	25.00	30.00

LOTUS, PATTERN #1921
Westmoreland Glass Co., 1921 – 1980
amber, amethyst, black, blue, crystal, green, milk, pink, red, and various applied color trims; sanitized colors

	Sanitized Colors	Other Colors		Sanitized Colors	Other Colors
6 Bowl, 6", lily (flat mayonnaise)	15.00	25.00	1 Lamp	195.00	350.00
Bowl, 9", cupped	50.00	85.00	Mayonnaise, 4", footed, flared rim	15.00	25.00
Bowl, 11", belled	60.00	95.00	Mayonnaise, 5", footed, bell rim	27.50	52.50
Bowl, oval vegetable	45.00	85.00	4 Plate, 6", mayonnaise	8.00	12.00
Candle, 4", single	18.00	35.00	2 Plate, 8½", salad	10.00	35.00
Candle, 9" high, twist stem	55.00	75.00	Plate, 8¾", mayonnaise	12.50	17.50
Candy jar with lid, ½ lb.	70.00	100.00	Plate, 13", flared	35.00	50.00
Coaster	12.00	15.00	Puff box, 5", with cover	110.00	145.00
Cologne, ½ oz.	90.00	110.00	Salt, individual	15.00	20.00
Comport, 2½", mint, twist stem	30.00	——	5 Shaker	30.00	45.00
Comport, 6½", honey	20.00	25.00	3 Sherbet, tulip bell	22.00	35.00
Comport, 5" high	30.00	40.00	Sugar	20.00	30.00
Comport, 8½" high, twist stem	60.00	85.00	Tray, lemon, 6", handle	30.00	40.00
Creamer	20.00	30.00	Tumbler, 10 oz.	——	50.00

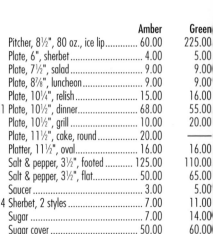

MADRID
Federal Glass Company, 1932 – 1939
green, pink, amber, crystal, "Madonna" blue
See Reproduction Section, Pages 206 – 207

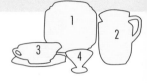

	Amber	Green
Ashtray, 6", sq.	450.00	450.00
Bowl, 4¾", cream soup	15.00	—
Bowl, 5", sauce	8.00	8.00
Bowl, 7", soup	15.00	15.00
Bowl, 8", salad	14.00	17.50
Bowl, 93/8", lg. berry	20.00	—
Bowl, 9½", deep salad	30.00	—
Bowl, 10", oval vegetable	20.00	22.00
Bowl, 11", low console	14.00	—
Butter dish & cover	70.00	90.00
Candlesticks, 2¼", pr.	22.00	—
Cookie jar & cover	50.00	—
Creamer, footed	10.00	11.00
Cup	6.00	9.00
Gelatin mold, 2⅛" high	9.00	—
3 Gravy boat & platter	2,000.00	—
Hot dish coaster	120.00	100.00
Hot dish coaster with indent	120.00	100.00
Jam dish, 7"	28.00	25.00
Pitcher, 5½", juice, 36 oz	42.00	—
2 Pitcher, 8", sq., 60 oz	50.00	140.00
Pitcher, 8½", 80 oz	60.00	200.00

	Amber	Green
Pitcher, 8½", 80 oz., ice lip	60.00	225.00
Plate, 6", sherbet	4.00	5.00
Plate, 7½", salad	9.00	9.00
Plate, 8⅞", luncheon	9.00	9.00
Plate, 10¼", relish	15.00	16.00
1 Plate, 10½", dinner	68.00	55.00
Plate, 10½", grill	10.00	20.00
Plate, 11½", cake, round	20.00	—
Platter, 11½", oval	16.00	16.00
Salt & pepper, 3½", footed	125.00	110.00
Salt & pepper, 3½", flat	50.00	65.00
Saucer	3.00	5.00
4 Sherbet, 2 styles	7.00	11.00
Sugar	7.00	14.00
Sugar cover	50.00	60.00
Tumbler, 3⅞", 5 oz.	15.00	32.00
Tumbler, 4¼", 9 oz.	16.00	20.00
Tumbler, 5½", 12 oz., 2 styles	20.00	30.00
Tumbler, 4", 5 oz., footed	45.00	40.00
Tumbler, 5½", 10 oz., footed	30.00	45.00
Wooden Lazy Susan, 7 hot dish coasters	1,225.00	—

MANHATTAN, "HORIZONTAL RIBBED"
Anchor Hocking Glass Company, 1939 – 1941
pink, crystal, green

	Crystal	Pink
Ashtray, 4", round	9.00	——
Ashtray, 4½", sq.	14.00	——
Bowl, 4½", sauce with handles	9.00	——
Bowl, 5⅜", berry with handles	18.00	20.00
Bowl, 5¼", cereal	110.00	225.00
Bowl, 7½", lg. berry	22.00	——
Bowl, 8", closed handles	25.00	28.00
Bowl, 9", salad	30.00	——
Bowl, 9½", fruit, open hndl.	35.00	45.00
Candlesticks, 4½", sq., pr.	18.00	——
Candy dish, 3 legs	——	15.00
Coaster, 3½"	15.00	——
1 Compote, 5¾"	35.00	45.00
5 Creamer, oval	11.00	15.00
Cup	12.00	300.00
2 Pitcher, 24 oz.	35.00	75.00

	Crystal	Pink
Pitcher, 80 oz., tilted	50.00	70.00
Plate, 6", sherbet	4.00	75.00
Plate, 8½", salad	15.00	——
Plate, 10¼", dinner	18.00	250.00
Plate, 14", sandwich	25.00	——
Relish tray, 14", 4-part	30.00	——
Relish tray, 14", 5-part	30.00	18.00
Relish tray insert	6.00	8.00
Salt & pepper, 2", sq., pr.	30.00	50.00
Saucer (same as 6" plate)	4.00	75.00
Sherbet	12.00	18.00
4 Sugar, oval	11.00	15.00
Tumbler, 10 oz., footed	18.00	25.00
3 Vase, 8"	25.00	——
Wine, 3½"	4.00	——

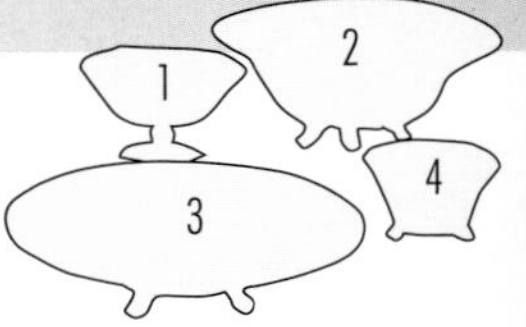

MAYA
Line #221, Paden City Glass Company, late 1930s – 1951; Canton Glass Co., 1950s
crystal, light blue, red

	Crystal	Colors		Crystal	Colors
Bowl, 7", flared rim	15.00	30.00	Comport, 6½" x 10", plain rim, pedestal	28.00	60.00
Bowl, 9½", non-flared	25.00	50.00	Creamer, flat	15.00	40.00
2 Bowl, 11⅝", 3½" deep, tri-footed, flared rim	30.00	70.00	Mayonnaise, tri-footed	15.00	35.00
3 Bowl, 12¾", 4¾" deep, tri-footed, flat rim	30.00	70.00	4 Mayonnaise, tri-footed, crimped	18.00	40.00
Cake plate, pedestal	35.00	70.00	Plate, 6⅝"	6.00	12.00
Candleholder	25.00	50.00	Plate, 7", mayonnaise	8.00	15.00
Candy, footed with lid, 3-part	40.00	90.00	Sugar, flat	15.00	40.00
Cheese dish with lid	60.00	150.00	Tray, 13¾", tri-footed, serving	25.00	60.00
1 Comport, fluted rim, pedestal	30.00	60.00	Tray, tab-hndl.	22.00	55.00

MAYFAIR FEDERAL
Federal Glass Company, 1934
crystal, amber, green

	Amber	Green		Amber	Green
Bowl, 5", sauce	7.00	11.00	2 Plate, 9½", dinner	12.00	14.00
Bowl, 5", cream soup	18.00	25.00	Plate, 9½", grill	15.00	15.00
Bowl, 6", cereal	18.00	22.00	Platter, 12", oval	28.00	32.00
Bowl, 10", oval vegetable	28.00	32.00	4 Saucer	2.00	3.00
Creamer, footed	11.00	14.00	Sugar, footed	11.00	18.00
Cup	7.00	9.00	Tumbler, 4½", 9 oz.	28.00	35.00
Plate, 6¾", salad	5.00	8.00			

MAYFAIR, "OPEN ROSE"
Hocking Glass Company, 1931 – 1937
pink, green, blue, yellow, crystal, satinized pink or blue
(See Reproduction Section, Pages 208 – 210)

	Pink	Blue
5 Bowl, 5", cream soup	55.00	—
6 Bowl, 5½", cereal	30.00	55.00
Bowl, 7", vegetable	30.00	55.00
Bowl, 9", 3⅛" high, 3-leg console	5,750.00	—
Bowl, 9½", oval vegetable	35.00	70.00
Bowl, 10", vegetable	30.00	70.00
Bowl, 10", same covered	145.00	150.00
Bowl, 11¾", low flat	60.00	70.00
Bowl, 12", deep scalloped fruit	65.00	100.00
Butter dish & cover or 7", covered vegetable	75.00	300.00
Cake plate, footed	32.00	65.00
3 Candy dish & cover	60.00	300.00
Celery dish, 10"	45.00	75.00
Celery dish, 10", divided	295.00	70.00
2 Cookie jar & lid	60.00	295.00
Creamer, footed	30.00	70.00
8 Cup	18.00	50.00

	Pink	Blue
Decanter & stopper, 32 oz.	210.00	—
Goblet, 4", cocktail, 3 oz.	110.00	—
Goblet, 4½", wine, 3 oz.	120.00	—
Goblet, 5¾", water, 9 oz	75.00	—
Goblet, 7¼", thin, 9 oz.	325.00	275.00
1 Pitcher, 6", 37 oz.	65.00	165.00
Pitcher, 8", 60 oz.	70.00	195.00
Pitcher, 8½", 80 oz.	125.00	240.00
7 Plate, 5¾" (often substituted as saucer)	13.00	17.50
Plate, 6½", round sherbet	14.00	—
Plate, 6½", round, off-center indent	22.00	30.00
Plate, 8½", luncheon	28.00	50.00
Plate, 9½", dinner	58.00	80.00
Plate, 9½", grill	50.00	60.00
Plate, 12", cake with hndl.	45.00	70.00
Platter, 12", oval, open hndl.	33.00	75.00
Relish, 8⅜", 4-part	35.00	70.00

Continued

	Pink	Blue
Relish, 8⅜", non-partitioned	225.00	——
Salt & pepper, flat, pr.	65.00	290.00
Salt & pepper, footed, pr.	10,000.00	——
Sandwich server/center hndl	50.00	80.00
Saucer (cup ring)	30.00	——
Saucer (see 5¾" plate)		
Sherbet, 2¼", flat	200.00	195.00
Sherbet, 3", footed	16.00	——
Sherbet, 4¾", footed	85.00	90.00
Sugar, footed	30.00	70.00
Sugar lid	2,995.00	——

	Pink	Blue
Tumbler, 3¼", juice, 3 oz., footed	95.00	——
Tumbler, 3½", juice, 5 oz.	55.00	125.00
Tumbler, 4¼", water, 9 oz.	35.00	105.00
Tumbler, 4¾", water, 11 oz.	225.00	150.00
Tumbler, 5¼", 10 oz., footed	40.00	155.00
Tumbler, 5¼", 13½ oz., iced tea	70.00	225.00
Tumbler, 6½", iced tea, 15 oz., footed	40.00	225.00
Vase (sweet pea)	195.00	125.00
Whiskey, 2¼", 1½ oz.	130.00	——

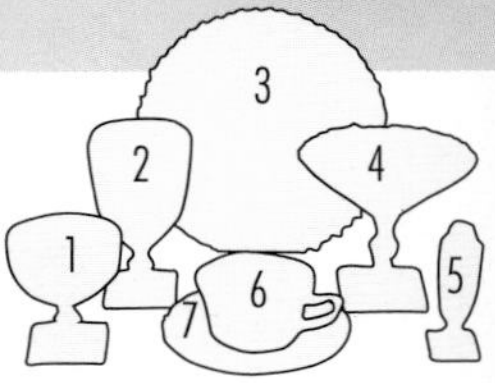

MISS AMERICA
Hocking Glass Company, 1933 – 1937
pink, green, crystal, red
See Reproduction Section, Pages 211 – 212

	Crystal	Pink
Bowl, 6¼", berry	9.00	25.00
Bowl, 8", curved in at top	40.00	100.00
Bowl, 8¾", straight, deep fruit	35.00	90.00
Bowl, 10", oval vegetable	15.00	45.00
Butter dish & cover	210.00	650.00
Cake plate, 12", footed	25.00	65.00
Candy jar & cover, 11½"	55.00	140.00
Celery dish, 10½", oblong	16.00	40.00
Coaster, 5¾"	16.00	35.00
4 Compote, 5"	15.00	35.00
Creamer, footed	11.00	23.00
6 Cup	8.00	22.00
Goblet, 3¾", wine, 3 oz.	22.00	120.00
Goblet, 4¾", juice, 5 oz.	25.00	115.00
2 Goblet, 5½", water, 10 oz.	18.00	52.00
Pitcher, 8", 65 oz.	50.00	165.00

	Crystal	Pink
Pitcher, 8½", 65 oz., with ice lip	70.00	195.00
Plate, 5¾", sherbet	5.00	11.00
Plate, 8½", salad	8.00	25.00
3 Plate, 10¼", dinner	16.00	40.00
Plate, 10¼", grill	11.00	30.00
Platter, 12", oval	15.00	42.00
Relish, 8¾", 4-part	11.00	22.00
Relish, 11¾", round, divided	25.00	6,750.00
5 Salt & pepper, pr.	35.00	68.00
7 Saucer	3.00	8.00
1 Sherbet	8.00	16.00
Sugar	9.00	22.00
Tumbler, 4", juice, 5 oz.	15.00	80.00
Tumbler, 4½", water, 10 oz.	12.00	38.00
Tumbler, 5¾", iced tea, 14 oz.	25.00	110.00

MODERNTONE, "WEDDING BAND"
Hazel Atlas Glass Company, 1934 – 1942
blue, amethyst, platonite fired-on colors

	Cobalt	Amethyst
Ashtray, 7¾", match holder in center	150.00	—
Bowl, 4¾", cream soup	18.00	18.00
Bowl, 5", berry	28.00	25.00
Bowl, 5", cream soup, ruffled	70.00	—
Bowl, 6½", cereal	95.00	75.00
Bowl, 7½", soup	165.00	100.00
Bowl, 8¾", lg. berry	50.00	40.00
Butter dish with metal cover	110.00	—
Cheese dish, 7" with metal lid	350.00	—
Creamer	12.00	10.00
Cup	10.00	8.00
Cup (no handle), custard	20.00	15.00
Plate, 5¾", sherbet	6.00	5.00
Plate, 6¾", salad	10.00	9.00

	Cobalt	Amethyst
Plate, 7¾", luncheon	11.00	10.00
Plate, 8⅞", dinner	15.00	12.00
1 Plate, 10½", sandwich	45.00	35.00
Platter, 11", oval	45.00	35.00
Platter, 12", oval	75.00	45.00
4 Salt & pepper, pr.	40.00	40.00
Saucer	3.00	3.00
5 Sherbet	10.00	10.00
Sugar	12.00	10.00
Sugar lid in metal	37.50	—
6 Tumbler, 5 oz	70.00	35.00
Tumbler, 9 oz	35.00	25.00
Tumbler, 12 oz	125.00	75.00
3 Whiskey, 1½ oz	35.00	—

MODERNTONE PLATONITE
Hazel Atlas Glass Company, 1940 – early 1950s

	Pastel Colors	Deco Red/Blue Willow		Pastel Colors	Deco Red/Blue Willow
Bowl, 4¾", cream soup	6.50	25.00	4 Metal lid, fits 5" bowl sold		
Bowl, 5", berry, with rim	5.00	15.00	w/cottage cheese	10.00	——
6 Bowl, 5", berry, without rim	6.00	——	Plate, 6¾", sherbet	4.00	11.00
3 Bowl, 5", deep cereal, with white	7.50	——	Plate, 8⅞", dinner	6.00	30.00
Bowl, 5", deep cereal, without white	10.00	——	Plate, 10½", sandwich	15.00	40.00
Bowl, 8", with rim	15.00*	45.00	Platter, 11", oval	——	40.00
Bowl, 8", without rim	25.00*	——	Platter, 12", oval	15.00**	50.00
Bowl, 8¾", lg. berry	——	45.00	Salt & pepper, pr.	16.00	——
Creamer	4.00	25.00	2 Saucer	1.00	5.00
1 Cup	3.50	25.00	5 Sherbet	4.00	22.00
			Sugar	4.00	25.00
*Pink $8.50			Tumbler, 9 oz.	9.00	——
**Yellow $8.00					

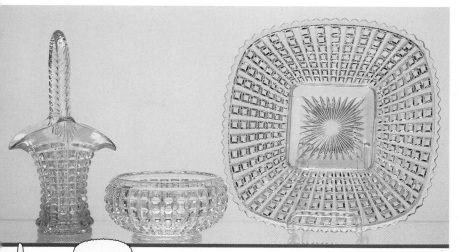

MONTICELLO, Later WAFFLE #698
Imperial Glass Co., circa 1920 – 1960s
crystal, Rubigold, milk, clambroth, teal

	Crystal
Basket, 10"	20.00
Bonbon, 5½", 1 hndl	11.00
Bowl, 4½", finger	10.00
Bowl, 4½", fruit, 2 styles	8.00
Bowl, 5", lily	18.00
Bowl, 5", fruit	10.00
Bowl, 5½", crème soup	12.50
Bowl, 6", lily	20.00
Bowl, 6", round	10.00
Bowl, 6½", belled	12.50
Bowl, 7", flower (with flower grid)	45.00
Bowl, 7", lily	28.00
Bowl, 7", nappy or round	12.50
Bowl, 7½", sq. or belled	15.00
Bowl, 8", lily (cupped)	35.00
Bowl, 8", round vegetable	22.00
Bowl, 8", round or shallow	17.00
Bowl, 8½", belled	17.50
Bowl, 9", round	20.00
Bowl, 9", shallow	17.50
Bowl, 10", belled	25.00
Bowl, 10", shallow	22.00
Bowl, 12", deep	30.00
Buffet set, 3-pc. (mayonnaise, spoon, 16½" round plate)	60.00
Butter tub, 5½"	35.00
Celery, 9", oval	20.00
Cheese dish and cover	65.00
Coaster, 3¼"	7.00
Compote, 5¼"	11.00

	Crystal
Compote, 5¾", belled rim	12.00
Creamer	11.00
Cup	9.00
Cuspidor	55.00
Mayonnaise set, 3-pc.	25.00
Pickle, 6", oval	15.00
Pitcher, 52 oz., ice lip	55.00
Plate, 6", bread	4.00
Plate, 8", salad	8.00
Plate, 9", dinner	18.00
Plate, 10½", sq.	22.00
Plate, 12", round	30.00
Plate, 16", cupped	45.00
Plate, 16½", round	45.00
Plate, 17", flat	45.00
Punch bowl, belled rim	55.00
Punch cup	7.00
Relish, 8¼", divided	15.00
Salt and pepper with glass tops	20.00
Saucer	3.00
Sherbet	9.00
Stem, cocktail	11.00
Stem, water	14.00
Sugar, open	11.00
Tidbit, 2-tier (7½" & 10½")	40.00
Tumbler, 9 oz., water	10.00
Tumbler, 12 oz., tea	12.00
Vase, 6"	22.50
Vase, 10½", flat	38.00

MOONDROPS
New Martinsville, 1932 – 1940s 
amber, pink, green, cobalt blue, ice blue, red, amethyst, crystal,
dark green, light green, jadite, smoke, black

	Red/Blue	Others		Red/Blue	Other
Ashtray	30.00	17.00	Cocktail shaker with or without		
Bowl, 4¼", cream soup	80.00	35.00	hndl., metal top	60.00	35.00
Bowl, 5¼", berry	25.00	12.00	1 Compote, 4"	27.50	18.00
Bowl, 6¾", soup	90.00	30.00	Compote, 11½"	85.00	52.00
Bowl, 7½", pickle	35.00	20.00	Creamer, 2¾", miniature	15.00	10.00
Bowl, 8⅜", footed, concave top	45.00	25.00	5 Creamer, 3¾", regular	15.00	9.00
Bowl, 8½", 3-footed, divided relish	45.00	20.00	7 Cup	15.00	10.00
Bowl, 9½", 3-legged, ruffled	60.00	—	Decanter, sm., 7¾"	70.00	40.00
Bowl, 9¾", oval vegetable	75.00	45.00	Decanter, med., 8½"	75.00	45.00
Bowl, 9¾", covered casserole	225.00	145.00	Decanter, lg., 11¼"	110.00	55.00
Bowl, 9¾", 2 hndl., oval	52.50	35.00	Decanter, "rocket," 10¼"	595.00	425.00
Bowl, 11½", celery, boat shaped	32.00	23.00	Goblet, 2⅞", ¾ oz., cordial	28.00	18.00
Bowl, 12", 3-footed, round			Goblet, 4", wine, 4 oz.	18.00	12.00
casserole	85.00	32.00	Goblet, 4¼", "rocket" wine	60.00	35.00
Bowl, 13", console with "wings"	120.00	42.00	Goblet, 4¾", 5 oz.	22.00	15.00
Butter dish & cover	400.00	225.00	Goblet, 5⅛", 3 oz., wine,		
4 Candles, 2", ruffled, pr.	45.00	25.00	metal stem	18.00	11.00
Candles, 4½", sherbet style, pr.	35.00	20.00	Goblet, 5½", 4 oz., wine,		
6 Candlesticks, 5", "wings," pr.	100.00	60.00	metal stem	20.00	11.00
Candlesticks, 5¼", triple light, pr.	150.00	95.00	3 Goblet, 6¼", water, 9 oz.,		
Candlesticks, 8½", metal stem, pr.	50.00	30.00	metal stem	27.50	16.00
Candy dish, 8", ruffled	40.00	20.00	Mug, 5⅛", 12 oz.	40.00	25.00

Continued

	Red/Blue	Others
Perfume bottle, "rocket"	295.00	195.00
Pitcher, sm., 6⅞", 22 oz.	150.00	75.00
Pitcher, med., 8⅛", 32 oz.	160.00	80.00
Pitcher, lg. with lip, 8", 50 oz.	170.00	85.00
Pitcher, lg., no lip, 8⅛", 53 oz.	165.00	85.00
Plate, 5⅞", bread & butter	11.00	8.00
Plate, 6⅛", sherbet	8.00	5.00
Plate, 6", round, off-center indent for sherbet	12.00	9.00
Plate, 7⅛", salad	14.00	10.00
Plate, 8½", luncheon	15.00	12.00
Plate, 9½", dinner	30.00	18.00
Plate, 14", round sandwich	40.00	18.00
Plate, 14", 2 hndl., sandwich	60.00	25.00
Platter, 12", oval	45.00	25.00
Powder jar w/lid, 3-footed	295.00	195.00
8 Saucer	4.00	3.00
Sherbet, 2⅝"	16.00	11.00

	Red/Blue	Others
Sherbet, 4½"	30.00	16.00
Sugar, 2¾"	12.00	10.00
Sugar, 4"	15.00	9.00
Tumbler, 2¾", hndl., shot, 2 oz.	20.00	12.00
Tumbler, 2¾", shot, 2 oz.	20.00	12.00
Tumbler, 3¾", juice, 3 oz., footed	18.00	11.00
Tumbler, 3⅝", 5 oz.	16.00	10.00
Tumbler, 4⅜", 7 oz.	16.00	10.00
2 Tumbler, 4⅜", 8 oz.	20.00	11.00
Tumbler, 4⅞", 9 oz.	21.00	15.00
Tumbler, 4⅞", hndl., 9 oz.	30.00	16.00
Tumbler, 5⅛", 12 oz.	30.00	15.00
Tray, 7½" for miniature sugar/creamer	28.00	16.00
Vase, 7¾", flat, ruffled top	60.00	50.00
Vase, 8½", "rocket," bud	295.00	175.00
Vase, 9¼", "rocket" style	295.00	150.00

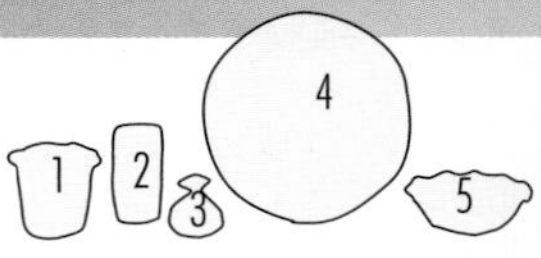

MOONSTONE
Anchor Hocking Glass Company, 1941 – 1946
crystal with opalescent hobnails
Pictured are experimental items only from Anchor-Hocking's Morgue.

	Opalescent
Bowl, 5½", berry	18.00
Bowl, 5½", crimped dessert	9.00
Bowl, 6½", crimped, hndl.	10.00
Bowl, 7¾", flat	11.00
Bowl, 7¾", divided relish	9.00
Bowl, 9½", crimped	28.00
Bowl, cloverleaf	14.00
Candleholder, pr.	18.00
Candy jar & cover, 6"	28.00
Cigarette jar & cover	22.00
Creamer	10.00

	Opalescent
Cup	6.00
Goblet, 10 oz.	20.00
Heart bonbon, 1 hndl.	15.00
Plate, 6¼", sherbet	4.00
Plate, 8", luncheon	12.00
Plate, 10¾", sandwich	25.00
Puff box & cover, 4¾", round	22.00
Saucer (same as sherbet plate)	4.00
Sherbet, footed	9.00
Sugar, footed	10.00
Vase, 5½", bud	18.00

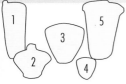

MOROCCAN AMETHYST
Hazel Ware, Division of Continental Can, 1960s
amethyst

	Amethyst
Ashtray, 3¼", triangular	6.00
Ashtray, 3¼", round	5.50
Ashtray, 6⅝", triangular	8.00
Ashtray, 8", sq.	13.00
Bowl, 4¾", fruit, octagonal	8.00
Bowl, 5¾", deep, sq.	10.00
Bowl, 6", round	10.00
Bowl, 7¾", oval	12.00
Bowl, 9¾", rectangular	14.00
Bowl, 9¾", rectangular, with metal hndl.	16.00
Bowl, 10¾"	25.00
Candy with lid, short	35.00
Candy with lid, tall	33.00
Chip and dip, 10¾" & 5¾", bowls in metal holder	35.00
Cocktail with stirrer, 6¼", 16 oz., with lip	32.00
Cocktail shaker, with lid	32.00
Cup	5.00
Goblet, 4", 4½ oz., wine	10.00

	Amethyst
Goblet, 4¼", 7½ oz., sherbet	8.00
Goblet, 4⅜", 5½ oz., juice	9.00
Goblet, 5½", 9 oz., water	10.00
3 Ice bucket, 6"	38.00
Plate, 5¾"	4.50
Plate, 7¼", salad	7.00
Plate, 9⅜", dinner	8.00
Plate, 10", fan-shaped, snack with cup rest	7.00
Plate, 12", sandwich with metal hndl.	17.50
Saucer	1.00
4 Tumbler, 2½", juice, 4 oz.	8.50
Tumbler, 3¼", old fashioned, 8 oz.	12.00
Tumbler, water, 9 oz.	10.00
Tumbler, 4¼", water, crinkled bottom, 11 oz.	10.00
Tumbler, 4⅝", water, 11 oz.	10.00
Tumbler, 6½", iced tea, 16 oz.	16.00
5 Vase, 8½", ruffled	32.00

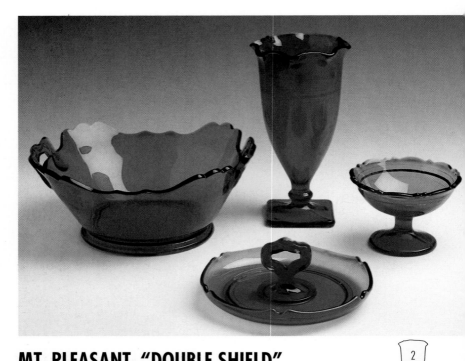

MT. PLEASANT, "DOUBLE SHIELD"
L.E. Smith Company, 1920s – 1934
black amethyst, amethyst, cobalt blue, green, pink

	Black Amethyst, Cobalt
Bonbon, rolled up handles, 7"	23.00
Bowl, 4", opening, rose	25.00
Bowl, 4", sq. fruit, footed	20.00
Bowl, 6", 2 hndl., sq.	18.00
Bowl, 7", 3-footed, rolled-out edge	25.00
Bowl, 8", scalloped, 2 hndl.	35.00
1 Bowl, 8", sq., 2 hndl.	35.00
Bowl, 9", scalloped, 1¾" deep, footed	35.00
Bowl, 9¼", sq. fruit, footed	33.00
Bowl, 10", scalloped fruit	45.00
Bowl, 10", 2 hndl., turned-up edge	35.00
Candlesticks, single, pr.	30.00
Candlesticks, double, pr.	45.00
Creamer	18.00
Cup (waffle-like crystal)	4.50
Cup	10.00
Leaf, 8"	15.00

	Black Amethyst, Cobalt
Leaf, 11¼"	30.00
Mayonnaise, 5½", 3-footed	25.00
4 Mint, 6", center handle	25.00
Plate, 7", 2 hndl., scalloped	13.00
Plate, 8", scalloped or sq.	15.00
Plate, 8", 2 hndl.	18.00
Plate, 8¼" sq. with indent for cup	16.00
Plate, 9", grill	20.00
Plate, 10½", cake, 2 hndl.	30.00
Plate, 12", 2 hndl.	32.00
Salt & pepper, 2 styles	50.00
Sandwich server, center hndl.	30.00
Saucer	3.00
3 Sherbet	16.00
Sugar	18.00
Tumbler, footed	22.00
2 Vase, 7¼"	32.00

MOUNT VERNON
Imperial Glass Co., Late 1920s – 1970s
(crystal, red, green, yellow, milk, iridized, red flash)

	Crystal
Basket, bowl, 9"	30.00
Bonbon, 5¾", 1 hndl.	10.00
Bowl, 5", finger	12.00
Bowl, 5¾", 2-handle	10.00
Bowl, 5¾", 2-handle, with cover	25.00
Bowl, 6", lily	15.00
Bowl, 7", lily	18.00
Bowl, 8", lily	20.00
Bowl, 10", console	25.00
Bowl, 10", 3-footed	28.00
Bowl, punch	35.00
Butter dish, 5"	35.00
Butter dish, dome top	40.00
Butter tub, 5"	15.00
Candlestick, 9"	28.00
Celery, 10½"	23.00
Creamer, individual	8.00
Creamer, lg.	12.00
Cup, coffee	8.00
Cup, custard or punch	8.00
Decanter	38.00
Oil bottle, 6 oz.	30.00
Pickle jar, with cover	35.00
Pickle, tall, 2 hndl.	22.00
Pickle, 6", 2 hndl.	18.00
Pitcher top, for 69 oz.	40.00

	Crystal
2 Pitcher, 54 oz.	37.50
Pitcher, 69 oz., straight edge	42.50
Plate, 6", bread & butter	4.00
Plate, 8", round	9.00
Plate, 8", sq.	9.00
Plate, 11", cake	18.00
Plate, 12½", sandwich	25.00
Plate, 13¼", torte	30.00
Plate, 18", liner for punch	35.00
Saucer	2.00
Shaker, pair	22.00
Spooner	22.00
Stem, 2 oz., wine	12.00
Stem, 3 oz., cocktail	8.00
Stem, 5 oz., sherbet	6.00
Stem, 9 oz., water goblet	9.00
Sugar lid, for individual	8.00
Sugar lid, for lg.	12.00
Sugar, individual	8.00
Sugar, lg.	12.00
Syrup, 8½ oz., with cover	50.00
Tidbit, 2-tier	30.00
Tumbler, 7 oz., old fashioned	10.00
1 Tumbler, 9 oz., water	8.00
Tumbler, 12 oz., iced tea	12.00
Vase, 10", orange bowl	50.00

NATIONAL
Jeannette Glass Co., late 1940s – mid 1950s
blue, crystal, pink, and Shell Pink

	Crystal
Ashtray, sm.	3.00
Ashtray, lg.	4.00
Bowl, 4½", berry	4.00
Bowl, 8½", lg. berry	15.00
Bowl, 12", flat	15.00
Candle, 3 footed	15.00
Candy, footed, with cover	22.50
Celery, 9½"	15.00
Cigarette box	12.50
Creamer	5.00
1 Cup	3.00
Jar, relish	12.50
Lazy Susan	45.00
Marmalade	15.00
Pitcher, 20 oz., milk	17.50
Pitcher, 64 oz.	27.50
Plate, 8", salad	5.00

	Crystal
4 Plate, 15", serving/punch liner	15.00
2 Punch bowl, 12"	25.00
3 Punch bowl stand	15.00
1 Punch cup	3.00
Punch set, 15-pc.	80.00
Relish, 13", 6-part	18.00
Saucer	1.00
Shakers, pr.	9.00
Sugar	5.00
Tray, 8", hndl., sugar/creamer	5.00
Tray, 12½", hndl.	15.00
Tumbler, 3¼", footed (go with)	4.00
Tumbler, 5", footed (go with)	5.00
Tumbler, 5¾", flat	8.00
Tumbler, 5½", flat	10.00
Tumbler, 7⅛", footed	12.50
Vase, 9"	20.00

NEW CENTURY, "LYDIA RAY"

Hazel Atlas Glass Company, 1930 – 1935

pink, green, crystal, amethyst, cobalt

		Green
5	Ashtray/coaster, 5⅜"	30.00
	Bowl, 4½", berry	35.00
	Bowl, 4¾", cream soup	22.00
	Bowl, 8", lg. berry	30.00
	Bowl, 9", covered casserole	100.00
	Butter dish & cover	60.00
	Cup	10.00
	Creamer	15.00
	Decanter & stopper	75.00
	Goblet, wine, 2½ oz.	35.00
	Goblet, cocktail, 3¼ oz.	35.00
	Pitcher, 7¾", 60 oz., with or without ice lip	35.00
	Pitcher, 8", 80 oz., with or without ice lip	40.00
	Plate, 6", sherbet	8.00
	Plate, 7⅛", breakfast	12.00
	Plate, 8½", salad	14.00

		Green
	Plate, 10", dinner	20.00
	Plate, 10", grill	20.00
	Platter, 11", oval	25.00
	Salt & pepper, pr.	38.00
	Saucer	3.00
6	Sherbet, 3"	12.00
	Sugar	10.00
7	Sugar cover	18.00
	Tumbler, 3½", 5 oz.	18.00
1	Tumbler, 4¼", 9 oz.	30.00
	Tumbler, 5", 10 oz.	22.00
2	Tumbler, 5¼", 12 oz.	33.00
	Tumbler, 4", 5 oz., footed	22.00
	Tumbler, 4⅞", 9 oz., footed	25.00
4	Whiskey, 2½", 1½ oz.	22.00

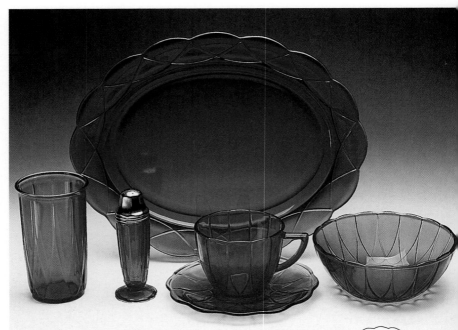

NEWPORT, "HAIRPIN"
Hazel Atlas Glass Company, 1936 – 1940
cobalt blue, amethyst, "Platonite" white and fired-on colors

	Cobalt	Fired-on Colors		Cobalt	Fired-on Colors
6 Bowl, 4¼", berry	18.00	7.50	Plate, 8¹³⁄₁₆", dinner	30.00	—
Bowl, 4¾", cream soup	18.00	10.00	Plate, 11½", sandwich	40.00	16.00
Bowl, 5¼", cereal	40.00	—	1 Platter, 11¾", oval	50.00	20.00
Bowl, 8¼", lg. berry	40.00	14.00	3 Salt & pepper	40.00	22.50
4 Cup	12.00	6.00	5 Saucer	4.00	1.00
Creamer	15.00	7.50	Sherbet	15.00	6.00
Plate, 5⅞", sherbet	8.00	1.50	Sugar	15.00	7.50
Plate, 8½", luncheon	16.00	5.00	2 Tumbler, 4½", 9 oz.	40.00	15.00

126

NORMANDIE, "BOUQUET AND LATTICE"
Federal Glass Company, 1933 – 1940
iridescent, amber, pink

	Amber	Pink
Bowl, 5", berry	9.00	9.00
Bowl, 6½", cereal	15.00	50.00
Bowl, 8½", lg. berry	25.00	40.00
Bowl, 10", oval vegetable	20.00	45.00
Creamer, footed	8.00	14.00
Cup	7.50	9.00
Pitcher, 8", 80 oz.	75.00	195.00
Plate, 6", sherbet	3.00	6.00
Plate, 7¾", salad	10.00	15.00
Plate, 9¼", luncheon	9.00	17.00
Plate, 11", dinner	30.00	150.00

		Amber	Pink
1	Plate, 11", grill	15.00	25.00
	Platter, 11¾"	22.00	50.00
	Salt & pepper, pr.	40.00	90.00
6	Saucer	2.00	3.00
3	Sherbet	6.00	10.00
4	Sugar	8.00	12.00
	Sugar lid	100.00	175.00
	Tumbler, 4", juice, 5 oz.	25.00	75.00
	Tumbler, 4¼", water, 9 oz.	20.00	55.00
	Tumbler, 5", iced tea, 12 oz.	35.00	110.00

NO. 610, "PYRAMID"
Indiana Glass Company, 1928 – 1932
green, pink, yellow, crystal; black and blue, 1974 – 1975 by Tiara

	Pink	Yellow		Pink	Yellow
Bowl, 4¾", berry	25.00	40.00	1 Pitcher	395.00	595.00
Bowl, 8½", master berry	55.00	75.00	2 Relish tray, 4-part, hndl.	60.00	65.00
3 Bowl, 9½", oval	40.00	65.00	Sugar	35.00	40.00
Bowl, 9½", pickle	35.00	55.00	Tray for creamer & sugar	30.00	55.00
4 Creamer	35.00	40.00	Tumbler, 8 oz., footed	55.00	90.00
Ice tub	135.00	225.00	Tumbler, 11 oz., footed	70.00	110.00
Ice tub lid	——	700.00			

NO. 612, "HORSESHOE"
Indiana Glass Company, 1930 – 1933
green, yellow, crystal

	Green	Yellow			Green	Yellow
Bowl, 4½", berry	30.00	25.00		Plate, 9⅜", luncheon	14.00	17.00
Bowl, 6½", cereal	32.00	35.00		Plate, 10⅜", grill	110.00	135.00
Bowl, 8½", vegetable	40.00	38.00	6	Plate, 11¼", sandwich	30.00	28.00
Bowl, 9½", lg. berry	50.00	50.00		Platter, 10¾", oval	32.00	35.00
Bowl, 10½", oval vegetable	30.00	33.00	1	Relish, 3-part, footed	30.00	40.00
Butter dish & cover	895.00	———		Saucer	4.00	4.00
Candy in metal holder, motif on			3	Sherbet	15.00	18.00
lid only	225.00	———	2	Sugar, open	16.00	17.00
Creamer, footed	16.00	17.00		Tumbler, 4¼", 9 oz.	185.00	———
Cup	11.00	12.00		Tumbler, 4¾"	195.00	———
Pitcher, 8½", 64 oz.	350.00	390.00		Tumbler, 9 oz., footed	32.00	32.00
Plate, 6", sherbet	7.00	7.00	4	Tumbler, 12 oz., footed	165.00	185.00
Plate, 8⅜", salad	13.00	13.00				

NO. 616, "VERNON"
Indiana Glass Company, 1930 – 1932
green, crystal, yellow

	Green	Yellow		Green	Yellow
4 Creamer, footed	25.00	25.00	Saucer	4.00	4.00
Cup	16.00	16.00	3 Sugar, footed	25.00	25.00
1 Plate, 8", luncheon	10.00	10.00	2 Tumbler, 5", footed	35.00	35.00
Plate, 11", sandwich	25.00	25.00			

NO. 618, "PINEAPPLE & FLORAL"
Indiana Glass Company, 1932 – 1937
crystal, amber, fired-on red

	Crystal	Amber
Ashtray, 4½"	15.00	——
Bowl, 4¾"	20.00	18.00
Bowl, 6", cereal	22.00	22.00
Bowl, 7", salad	2.00	10.00
Bowl, 10", oval vegetable	20.00	18.00
Compote, diamond shaped	1.00	10.00
Creamer, diamond shaped	8.00	10.00
Cream soup	18.00	22.00
Cup	8.00	10.00
Plate, 6", sherbet	3.00	5.00
Plate, 8⅜", salad	7.00	8.50

		Crystal	Amber
1	Plate, 9⅜", dinner	13.00	15.00
	Plate, 11½", sandwich	20.00	18.00
	Platter, 11", closed hndl.	15.00	18.00
	Platter, relish, 11½", divided	20.00	——
2	Saucer	3.00	4.00
	Sherbet, footed	13.00	18.00
	Sugar, diamond-shaped	8.00	10.00
3	Tumbler, 4¼", 8 oz.	25.00	——
	Tumbler, 5", 12 oz.	38.00	——
	Vase, cone shaped, lg.	55.00	——
	Vase holder, metal	35.00	——

NO. 622, "PRETZEL"
Indiana Glass Company, 1930s
crystal, teal

	Crystal
Bowl, 4½", fruit cup	3.00
Bowl, 7", olive, leaf-shaped	4.00
Bowl, 7½", soup	10.00
Bowl, 8½", 2 hndl., pickle	4.00
Bowl, 9⅜", berry	14.00
Bowl, 10¼", celery	2.00
Creamer	5.00
Cup	5.00
1 Pitcher, 39 oz.	495.00
Plate, 6", bread & butter	2.50

	Crysta
Plate, 6", tab hndl.	2.0(
Plate, 8⅜", salad	6.0(
Plate, 9⅜", dinner	10.0(
Plate, 11½", sandwich	11.0(
Saucer	1.0(
Sugar	5.0(
2 Tumbler, juice, 5 oz.	40.0(
Tumbler, water, 9 oz.	35.0(
3 Tumbler, 12 oz.	60.0(

OLD CAFE
Hocking Glass Company, 1936 – 1938; 1940
pink, crystal, ruby red

	Pink	Red		Pink	Red
Bowl, 3¾", berry, tab hndl.	8.00	9.00	Pitcher, 80 oz.	185.00	—
Bowl, 5", 1 or 2 hndl.	12.00	—	2 Plate, 6", sherbet	8.00	—
Bowl, 5½", cereal	35.00	35.00	1 Plate, 10", dinner	55.00	—
Bowl, 9", closed hndl.	30.00	—	Saucer	4.00	—
Candy dish, 8", low	14.00	8.00	Sherbet, low footed	15.00	12.00
Cup	12.00	12.00	Tumbler, 3", juice	12.00	20.00
Lamp	100.00	150.00	3 Tumbler, 4", water	20.00	30.00
Olive dish, 6", oblong	8.00	—	Vase, 7¼"	50.00	55.00
Pitcher, 6", 36 oz.	150.00	—			

OLD COLONY
Hocking Glass Company, 1935 – 1938
pink, crystal

	Pink
Bowl, 6⅜", cereal	22.00
Bowl, 7¾", salad	25.00
Bowl, 9½", plain or ribbed	25.00
Bowl, 10½", 3 legs	275.00
2 Butter dish or bonbon with cover	70.00
5 Candlesticks, pr.	450.00
Candy jar & cover, ribbed	50.00
Compote, 7"	28.00
Compote & cover, footed	65.00
4 Cookie jar & cover	85.00
Creamer	22.00
Cup	22.00
Fish bowl, 1 gal., 80 oz. (crystal only)	50.00
Flower bowl, crystal frog	35.00

	Pink
Plate, 7¼", salad	22.00
Plate, 8¾", luncheon	20.00
1 Plate, 10½", dinner	30.00
Plate, 10½", grill	22.00
Plate, 13", 4-part solid lace	60.00
Platter, 12¾"	40.00
Platter, 12¾", 5-part	35.00
Relish dish, 7½" deep, 3-part	85.00
Saucer	8.00
Sherbet, footed	125.00
Sugar	22.00
3 Tumbler, 4½", 9 oz., flat	20.00
Tumbler, 5", 10½ oz., footed	90.00
Vase, 7"	795.00

OLD ENGLISH, "THREADING"
Indiana Glass Company, Late 1920s
green, pink, amber

	All Colors		All Colors
2 Bowl, 4", berry	25.00	Pitcher	95.00
1 Bowl, 9", footed fruit	35.00	4 Pitcher with cover	155.00
Bowl, 9½", flat	38.00	Plate, indent for compote	20.00
Candlesticks, 4", pr.	40.00	Sandwich server, center hndl.	55.00
Candy jar with lid, footed	65.00	Sherbet, two styles	22.00
Candy & lid, flat	65.00	Sugar	18.00
Compote, 3½" tall, 7" across	25.00	Sugar cover	40.00
Compote, 3½" tall, 2-handled	22.00	5 Tumbler, 4½", footed	25.00
3 Compote, 3½" tall, ruffled	30.00	Tumbler, 5½", footed	35.00
Creamer	20.00	Vase, fan, 7"	75.00
Fruit stand, 11", footed	45.00	Vase, 12", footed	85.00
Goblet, 5¾", 8 oz.	30.00		

ORANGE BLOSSOM
LINE #619, Indiana Glass Co., circa 1957
milk white

	White
Bowl, 5½", dessert	4.00
7 Creamer, footed	4.00
6 Cup	2.00
1 Plate, 5¾", sherbet	2.00

	White
2 Plate, 8⅞", lunch	5.00
5 Saucer	.75
4 Sugar, footed	4.00

"ORCHID"
Paden City Glass Company, early 1930s
amber, blue, crystal, green, pink, red, yellow, black

	Red/Blue
Bowl, 4⅞", sq.	55.00
Bowl, 8½", 2 hndl.	135.00
Bowl, 8¾" sq.	135.00
Bowl, 10", footed	195.00
Bowl, 11", sq.	195.00
Candlesticks, 5¾", pr.	210.00
Candy with lid, 6½", sq., 3 pt.	195.00
Comport, 3¼" tall, 6¼" wide	55.00
Comport, 4¾" tall, 7⅜"wide	100.00
Comport, 6⅝" tall, 7" wide	135.00

	Red/Blue
Creamer	110.00
Ice bucket, 6"	195.00
Mayonnaise, 3-pc.	150.00
Plate, 8½", sq.	100.00
3 Sandwich server, center hndl.	100.00
Sugar	110.00
Vase, 8"	250.00
Vase, 10"	275.00

OVIDE, "INFORMAL"
Hazel Atlas Glass Company, 1930 – 1935
green, white, black

	Green	Decorated White			Green	Decorated White
Bowl, 4¾", berry	——	8.00	Plate, 6", sherbet	2.00	6.00
Bowl, 5½", cereal	——	13.00	1 Plate, 8", luncheon	3.00	14.00
Bowl, 8", lg. berry	——	22.50	Salt & pepper, pr.	28.00	24.00
Candy dish & cover	22.50	35.00	3 Saucer	2.00	6.00
Cocktail, fruit, footed	4.00	——	Sherbet	3.00	14.00
4 Creamer	4.00	17.50	5 Sugar, open	4.00	17.50
2 Cup	3.50	12.50	Tumbler	——	18.00
Egg cup	——	18.00			

OYSTER AND PEARL
Anchor Hocking Glass, 1938 – 1940
pink, crystal, ruby red, white with fired-on pink or green

	Pink	Red		Pink	Red
Bowl, 5¼", round or hndl.	——	22.00	2 Candleholder, 3½", pr.	35.00	65.00
Bowl, 5¼", heart-shaped, 1 hndl.	14.00	——	Plate, 13½", sandwich	20.00	55.00
Bowl, 6½" deep, hndl.	18.00	27.50	1 Relish dish, 10¼", oblong	20.00	——
Bowl, 10½", fruit, deep	25.00	60.00			

"PARK AVE."
Federal Glass Company, 1941 – Early 1970s

	Crystal	Yellow
Ashtray, 3½", sq.	4.00	——
Ashtray, 4½", sq.	6.00	——
6 Bowl, 5", dessert	2.00	7.00
4 Bowl, 8½", vegetable	10.00	18.00
5 Candleholder, 5"	8.00	——

	Crystal	Yellow
Tumbler, 2⅛", 1¼ oz., whiskey	4.00	——
Tumbler, 3½", 4½ oz., juice	4.00	6.00
3 Tumbler, 3⅞", 9 oz.	4.00	8.00
Tumbler, 4¾", 10 oz.	5.00	12.00
1 Tumbler, 5⅛", 12 oz., iced tea	6.00	15.00

"PARROT," SYLVAN
Federal Glass Company, 1931 – 1932
green, amber, crystal

	Green	Amber
Bowl, 5", berry	30.00	20.00
Bowl, 7", soup	50.00	35.00
Bowl, 8", lg. berry	100.00	90.00
Bowl, 10", oval veg.	60.00	65.00
Butter dish & cover	450.00	1,500.00
Creamer, footed	50.00	85.00
Cup	35.00	40.00
Hot plate, 5"	895.00	995.00
Jam dish, 7"	——	38.00
Pitcher, 8½", 80 oz.	3,000.00	——
Plate, 5¾", sherbet	25.00	20.00
Plate, 7½", salad	35.00	——
Plate, 9", dinner	55.00	45.00

	Green	Amber
Plate, 10½", grill, round	30.00	——
Plate, 10½", grill, sq.	——	30.00
Platter, 11¼", oblong	50.00	75.00
Salt & pepper, pr.	250.00	——
Saucer	12.50	15.00
Sherbet, footed, cone	20.00	23.00
Sherbet, 4¼" high	1,500.00	——
Sugar	35.00	50.00
Sugar cover	175.00	550.00
5 Tumbler, 4¼", 10 oz.	195.00	135.00
Tumbler, 5½", 12 oz.	200.00	150.00
3 Tumbler, 5¾", footed, heavy	175.00	165.00

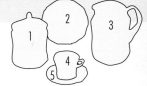

PATRICIAN, "SPOKE"
Federal Glass Company, 1933 – 1937
pink, green, amber, crystal

	Amber	Green		Amber	Green
Bowl, 4¾", cream soup	14.00	20.00	Plate, 9", luncheon	11.00	15.00
Bowl, 5", berry	12.00	11.00	Plate, 10½", dinner	8.00	40.00
Bowl, 6", cereal	20.00	30.00	Plate, 10½", grill	12.00	20.00
Bowl, 8½", lg. berry	35.00	35.00	Platter, 11½", oval	25.00	30.00
Bowl, 10", oval vegetable	30.00	35.00	Salt & pepper, pr.	50.00	80.00
Butter dish & cover	90.00	125.00	5 Saucer	6.00	7.50
1 Cookie jar & cover	80.00	695.00	Sherbet	8.00	14.00
Creamer, footed	10.00	15.00	Sugar	8.00	15.00
4 Cup	7.00	14.00	Sugar cover	60.00	85.00
Pitcher, 8", 75 oz.	135.00	165.00	Tumbler, 4", 5 oz.	28.00	30.00
3 Pitcher, 8¼", 75 oz.	——	175.00	Tumbler, 4½", 9 oz.	25.00	30.00
Plate, 6", sherbet	8.00	10.00	Tumbler, 5½", 14 oz.	40.00	50.00
2 Plate, 7½", salad	12.00	15.00	Tumbler, 5½", 8 oz., footed	55.00	70.00

"PATRICK"
Lancaster Glass Company, Early 1930s
yellow, pink

	Yellow	Pink		Yellow	Pink
Bowl, 9", fruit, hndl.	110.00	145.00	Mayonnaise, 3-pc.	140.00	175.00
Bowl, 11", console	110.00	135.00	Plate, 7", sherbet	8.00	12.00
Candlesticks, pr.	130.00	160.00	Plate, 7½", salad	12.00	17.50
Candy dish, 3-footed	225.00	225.00	1 Plate, 8", luncheon	16.00	25.00
Cheese & cracker set	110.00	125.00	7 Saucer	7.00	12.00
Creamer	25.00	40.00	Sherbet, 4¾"	50.00	60.00
Cup	25.00	35.00	5 Sugar	25.00	40.00
Goblet, 4", cocktail	80.00	80.00	Tray, 11", 2 hndl.	50.00	65.00
Goblet, 4¾", juice, 6 oz.	65.00	70.00	Tray, 11", center hndl.	100.00	125.00
Goblet, 6", water, 10 oz.	60.00	60.00			

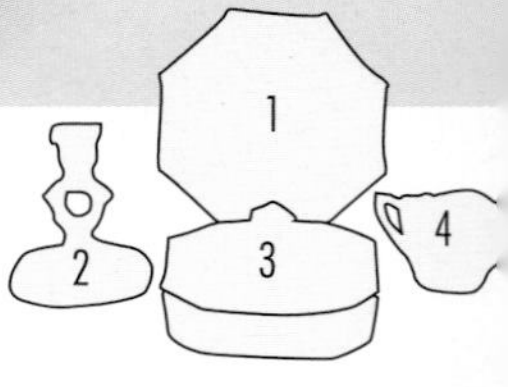

"PEACOCK REVERSE," "DELILAH BIRD"
Line #412, Paden City Glass Company, 1930s
amber, black, crystal, cobalt blue, green, pink, red, yellow

	All Colors
Bowl, 4⅞", sq.	50.00
Bowl, 8¾", sq.	125.00
Bowl, 8¾", sq. with hndl.	125.00
Bowl, 11¾", console	150.00
2 Candlesticks, 5¾", sq. base, pr.	175.00
3 Candy dish, 6½", sq.	195.00
Comport, 3¼" high, 6¼" wide	75.00
Comport, 4¼" high, 7⅜" wide	85.00
Creamer, 2¾", flat	125.00
Cup	155.00

	All Colors
Plate, 5¾", sherbet	22.00
1 Plate, 8½", luncheon	60.00
Plate 10⅜", 2 hndl.	100.00
Saucer	45.00
Sherbet, 4⅝" tall, 3⅜" diam.	75.00
Server, center hndl.	80.00
4 Sugar, 2¾", flat	125.00
Tumbler, 4", 10 oz. flat	100.00
Vase, 10"	250.00

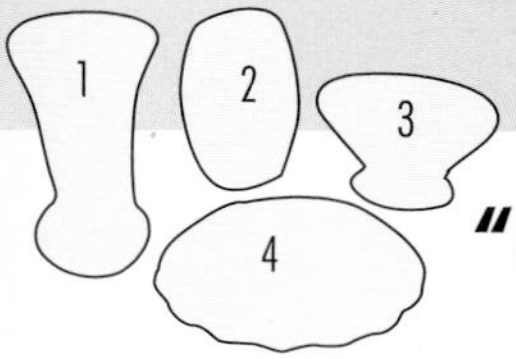

"PEACOCK & WILD ROSE," "NORA BIRD"
Line #300, Paden City Glass Company, 1930s
amber, white, cobalt blue, black, green, pink, red

	All Colors
Bowl, 8½", flat	135.00
Bowl, 8½", fruit, oval, footed	195.00
Bowl, 8¾", footed	175.00
Bowl, 9½", center hndl.	165.00
Bowl, 9½", footed	185.00
Bowl, 10½", center hndl.	125.00
Bowl, 10½", footed	195.00
Bowl, 10½", fruit	180.00
Bowl, 11", console	185.00
Bowl, 14", console	195.00
Candlestick, 5", pr.	150.00
Candy dish with cover, 6½", 3-part	195.00
Candy with lid, footed, 5¼" high	195.00
Candy dish with cover, 7"	250.00
Cheese & cracker set	195.00
Comport, 3¼" tall, 6¼" wide	135.00
Creamer, 4½", round hndl.	65.00
Creamer, 5", pointed hndl.	65.00
Cup	80.00

	All Colors
Ice bucket, 6"	225.00
Ice tub, 4¾"	210.00
Ice tub, 6"	225.00
Mayonnaise and liner	135.00
Pitcher, 5" high	395.00
Plate, 8"	25.00
Plate, cake, low foot	150.00
Relish, 3-part	125.00
Saucer	20.00
Sugar, 4½", round hndl.	65.00
Sugar, 5", pointed hndl.	65.00
Tumbler, 2¼", 3 oz.	65.00
Tumbler, 3"	75.00
Tumbler, 4"	95.00
Tumbler, 4¾", footed	110.00
Tumbler, 5¼", 10 oz.	110.00
2 Vase, 8¼", elliptical	395.00
1 Vase, 10", 2 styles	250.00
Vase, 12"	295.00

PETALWARE
MacBeth-Evans Glass Company, 1930 – 1940
pink, crystal, monax, cremax

	Pink	Monax		Pink	Monax
Bowl, 4½", cream soup	16.00	12.00	2 Plate, 8", salad	6.00	5.00
Bowl, 5¾", cereal	15.00	9.00	Plate, 9", dinner	16.00	14.00
Bowl, 9", lg. berry	20.00	20.00	1 Plate, 11", salver	15.00	12.00
5 Cup	7.00	5.00	Platter, 13", oval	25.00	15.00
Creamer, footed	8.00	7.00	4 Saucer	2.00	1.00
Lamp shade (many sizes)	——	8.00	6 Sherbet, low, footed	10.00	8.00
Mustard with metal cover in cobalt blue only	——	10.00	Sugar, footed	8.00	7.00
Plate, 6", sherbet	3.00	2.00	3 Tumbler, crystal, decorated	——	12.50

PILLAR OPTIC
Anchor Hocking Glass Co. (#2 possibly Federal Glass Co.),
1937 – 1942
crystal, green, pink, Royal Ruby

	Green/ Pink	Royal Ruby		Green/ Pink	Royal Ruby
Bowl, 9", 2 hndl.	65.00	150.00	Sugar, footed	65.00	100.00
Creamer, footed	65.00	100.00	Tumbler, 1½ oz., whiskey	15.00	—
Cup	12.00	75.00	Tumbler, 7 oz., old-fashioned	25.00	—
Mug, 12 oz.	35.00	—	Tumbler, 9 oz., water	15.00	—
Pitcher with lip, 80 oz.	45.00	—	Tumbler, 11 oz., footed, cone	20.00	—
Pitcher without lip, 60 oz.	45.00	—	Tumbler, 13 oz., tea	25.00	—
Plate, 8", luncheon	10.00	30.00	Tumbler, 3¼", 3 oz., footed	15.00	30.00
Pretzel jar, 130 oz.	150.00	—	Tumbler, 4", 5 oz., juice,		
Saucer	4.00	25.00	footed	18.00	50.00
Sherbet, ftd.	10.00	35.00	Tumbler, 5¼", 10 oz., footed	25.00	60.00

PRIMO, "PANELLED ASTER"
U.S. Company, Early 1930s
green, yellow

	Yellow/Green
Bowl, 4½"	25.00
Bowl, 7¾"	40.00
6 Bowl, 11", 3-footed	50.00
Cake plate, 10", 3-footed	75.00
7 Coaster/ashtray	8.00
Creamer	14.00
Cup	12.00
5 Plate, 6¼", sherbet	15.00

	Yellow/Gree
2 Plate, 7½"	14.0
Plate, 10", dinner	30.0
1 Plate, 10", grill	18.0
Plate, 10", grill w/indent	25.0
Saucer	3.0
4 Sherbet	14.0
Sugar	14.0
3 Tumbler, 5¾", 9 oz.	22.0

PRINCESS
Hocking Glass Company, 1931 – 1935
green, pink, topaz, apricot, some blue

	Pink	Green		Pink	Green
Ashtray, 4½"	95.00	80.00	Plate, 9½", dinner	22.00	25.00
Bowl, 4½", berry	32.00	32.00	Plate, 9½", grill	20.00	20.00
Bowl, 5", cereal or oatmeal	38.00	38.00	Plate, 10¼", sandwich, hndl.	30.00	30.00
Bowl, 9", salad, octagonal	50.00	45.00	Plate, 10½", grill, closed hndl.	12.00	12.00
Bowl, 9½", hat-shaped	50.00	50.00	Platter, 12", closed hndl.	30.00	30.00
Bowl, 10", oval vegetable	25.00	28.00	Relish, 7½", divided	30.00	30.00
Butter dish & cover	135.00	100.00	Relish, 7½", plain	200.00	200.00
Cake stand, 10", 3-footed	30.00	30.00	Salt & pepper, 4½", pr.	50.00	50.00
1 *Candy dish & cover	85.00	60.00	Saucer (same as sherbet plate)	6.00	6.00
Coaster	80.00	55.00	Sherbet, footed	22.00	20.00
Cookie jar & cover	70.00	55.00	Sugar	15.00	10.00
Creamer, oval	18.00	15.00	Sugar cover	20.00	25.00
Cup	10.00	10.00	Tumbler, 3", juice, 5 oz.	35.00	33.00
Pitcher, 6", 37 oz	75.00	65.00	Tumbler, 4", water, 9 oz.	30.00	28.00
Pitcher, 7⅜", 24 oz., footed	450.00	500.00	Tumbler, 5¼", iced tea, 13 oz.	45.00	50.00
Pitcher, 8", 60 oz	65.00	60.00	Tumbler, 4¾", 9 oz., sq. foot	60.00	65.00
Plate, 5½", sherbet	6.00	6.00	Tumbler, 5¼", 10 oz., footed	26.00	33.00
Plate, 8", salad	15.00	15.00	Tumbler, 6½", 12½ oz., footed	100.00	120.00
* Recently reproduced — Beware!			Vase, 8"	60.00	45.00

QUEEN MARY, "VERTICAL RIBBED"
Hocking Glass Company, 1936 – 1940
pink, crystal

	Pink	Crystal
Ashtray, 2" x 3¾", oval	6.00	4.00
Bowl, 4", 1 hndl. or none	5.00	4.00
Bowl, 5", berry	9.00	5.00
Bowl, 6", cereal	22.00	7.00
Bowl, 5½", 2 hndl.	18.00	6.00
Bowl, 8¾", lg. berry	25.00	15.00
2 Butter dish or preserve & cover	150.00	35.00
Candy dish & cover	65.00	20.00
3 Candlesticks, 4½", double branch, pr.	——	22.00
Celery or pickle dish, 5" x 10"	50.00	16.00
Cigarette jar, oval, 2" x 3"	8.00	6.00
Coaster, 3½"	9.00	5.00
Coaster/ashtray, 4¼", sq.	6.00	5.00
Compote, 5¾"	25.00	15.00
4 Creamer, footed	60.00	25.00
Creamer, oval	14.00	7.00

	Pink	Crystal
Cup	6.00	4.00
Plate, 6" & 6⅝"	5.00	4.00
Plate, 8½", salad	——	6.00
Plate, 9¾", dinner	55.00	25.00
Plate, 12", sandwich	28.00	18.00
Plate, 14", serving tray	22.00	12.00
Relish tray, 12", 3-part	——	15.00
Relish tray, 14", 4-part	——	15.00
Salt & pepper, pr.	——	20.00
Saucer	2.00	1.50
5 Sherbet, footed	12.00	5.00
6 Sugar, footed	60.00	25.00
Sugar, oval	14.00	7.00
Tumbler, 3½", juice, 5 oz.	13.00	4.00
Tumbler, 4", water, 9 oz.	15.00	6.00
1 Tumbler, 5", 10 oz., footed	65.00	30.00

RADIANCE
New Martinsville, 1936 – 1939
red, cobalt and ice blue, amber, crystal

	Red/Blue	Amber		Red/Blue	Amber
Bonbon, 6"	33.00	15.00	Cruet, individual	80.00	45.00
Bonbon, 6", footed	35.00	17.50	Cup	20.00	12.00
Bonbon, 6", covered	115.00	55.00	Decanter, hndl., with stopper	225.00	125.00
Bowl, 5", 2 hndl., nut	22.00	12.00	4 Goblet, 1 oz. cordial	25.00	10.00
Bowl, 7", 2-part	35.00	20.00	Lamp, 12"	125.00	65.00
5 Bowl, 7", pickle	35.00	20.00	Mayonnaise, 3-pc. set	115.00	65.00
Bowl, 8", 3-part, relish	40.00	35.00	2 Pitcher, 64 oz.	325.00	175.00
Bowl, 10", celery	45.00	22.00	Plate, 8", luncheon	20.00	10.00
Bowl, 10", crimped	55.00	30.00	Plate, 14", punch bowl liner	85.00	45.00
Bowl, 10", flared	50.00	25.00	Punch bowl	225.00	125.00
Bowl, 12", crimped	60.00	35.00	Punch cup, flat	15.00	7.00
Bowl, 12", flared	65.00	32.00	Punch ladle	150.00	100.00
Butter dish	450.00	210.00	Salt & pepper, pr.	95.00	40.00
Candlestick, 8", pr.	225.00	95.00	Saucer	8.50	5.00
Candle, 2-light, pr.	175.00	95.00	Sugar	25.00	15.00
3 Cheese & cracker, 11" plate set	125.00	35.00	Tray, oval	45.00	25.00
Comport, 5"	35.00	18.00	1 Tumbler, 9 oz.	34.00	22.00
Comport, 6"	38.00	22.00	Vase, 10", flared	110.00	75.00
Condiment set, 4-pc. on tray	325.00	175.00	Vase, 12", crimped	175.00	——
Creamer	25.00	15.00			

RAINBOW
Anchor Hocking Glass Co., 1938 – early 1950s
primary: tangerine, blue, green, yellow; pastel: pink, blue, green, and yellow

	Pastel*	Primary		Pastel*	Primary
Bowl, 5¼", utility, deep	——	15.00	1 Plate, 7¼", salad	8.00	10.00
Bowl 6", fruit	18.00	22.00	Plate, 9¼", dinner	12.00	14.00
Bowl, 9½", vegetable	——	65.00	Platter, 11"	——	65.00
3 Creamer, footed	12.50	12.00	Saucer	3.00	3.00
Cup	7.00	7.00	Shakers, pr.	——	25.00
**Jug, 42 oz., ball	70.00	85.00	2 Sherbet, footed	12.00	12.00
Jug, 42 oz., Manhattan	65.00	55.00	5 Sugar, footed	15.00	12.00
Jug, 54 oz.	——	60.00	Tumbler, 5 oz., fruit juice	——	12.00
Jug, 64 oz.	——	65.00	Tumbler, 9 oz., bath, straight	——	12.00
***Jug, 80 oz., ball	75.00	95.00	Tumbler, 9 oz., table	12.00	8.00
Jug, 80 oz., ball, Pillar Optic	——	80.00	4 Tumbler, 15 oz., footed	——	15.00
Plate, 6¼", sherbet	8.00	12.00	Tumbler, 12 oz., 4¾", straight	——	35.00

*Add 25% for green.   **Tangerine (red) $30.00   ***Tangerine $20.00

RAINDROPS, "OPTIC DESIGN"
Federal Glass Company, 1929 – 1933
green, crystal

	Green
Bowl, 4½", fruit	7.00
Bowl, 6", cereal	14.00
Bowl, 7½", berry	60.00
Cup	9.00
Creamer	8.00
3 Plate, 6", sherbet	3.00
Plate, 8", luncheon	8.00
Salt & pepper, pr.	425.00
Saucer	2.00
4 Sherbet	8.00

	Green
Sugar	7.00
Sugar/cover	40.00
6 Tumbler, 2⅛", 2 oz	5.00
Tumbler, 3", 4 oz.	5.00
1 Tumbler, 3⅞", 5 oz.	6.50
2 Tumbler, 4⅛", 9½ oz.	9.00
Tumbler, 5", 10 oz.	9.00
Tumbler, 5⅜", 14 oz	14.00
5 Whiskey, 1⅞"	7.00

RIBBON
Hazel Atlas Glass Company, 1930 – 1932
green, black, crystal

	Green	Black		Green	Black
Bowl, 4", berry	35.00	——	Plate, 6¼", sherbet	6.00	——
3 Bowl, 5", cereal	45.00	——	Plate, 8", luncheon	9.00	14.00
1 Bowl, 8", lg. berry	80.00	40.00	Saucer	2.00	——
Candy dish & cover	65.00	——	Sherbet, footed	10.00	——
4 Creamer, footed	13.00	——	2 Sugar, footed	12.00	——
Cup	5.00	——	Tumbler, 6", 10 oz.	37.50	——

RING, "BANDED RINGS"
Hocking Glass Company, 1927 – 1932
crystal, green and crystal with decoration

	Crystal	Green & Crystal w/dec.		Crystal	Green & Crystal w/dec.
1 Bowl, 5¼", divided	12.00	40.00	Plate, 8", luncheon	4.00	7.00
Bowl, 5", berry	4.00	8.00	Salt & pepper, 3", pr.	25.00	55.00
Bowl, 7", soup	10.00	15.00	Sandwich server, center hndl.	18.00	28.00
Bowl, 8", lg. berry	8.00	15.00	Saucer	1.50	2.00
Butter tub or ice tub	25.00	40.00	6 Sherbet, low (for 6½" plate)	8.00	15.00
Cocktail shaker	20.00	30.00	2 Sherbet, 4¾", footed	5.00	11.00
Cup	6.00	10.00	Sugar, footed	5.00	10.00
Creamer, footed	5.00	10.00	5 Tumbler, 3½", 5 oz.	5.00	12.00
Decanter & stopper	28.00	45.00	4 Tumbler, 4¼", 9 oz.	5.00	15.00
Goblet, 7" to 8" (varies), 9 oz.	14.00	20.00	Tumbler, 5⅛", 12 oz.	8.00	14.00
Ice bucket	20.00	40.00	Tumbler, 3½", footed cocktail	6.00	12.00
3 Pitcher, 8", 60 oz.	17.50	35.00	Tumbler, 5½", water, footed	6.00	12.00
Pitcher, 8½", 80 oz.	22.00	45.00	Tumbler, 6½", iced tea, footed	10.00	18.00
Plate, 6¼", sherbet	2.00	3.00	Vase, 8"	17.50	38.00
7 Plate, 6½", off-center ring	5.00	10.00	Whiskey, 2", 1½ oz.	7.00	15.00

RIPPLE, "CRINOLINE," "PETTICOAT," "PIE CRUST," "LASAGNA"

Hazel Atlas Glass Co., Early 1950s
platonite white, white with blue or pink trim

	All Colors
7 Bowl, berry, shallow, 5"	14.00
8 Bowl, cereal, deep, 5⅝"	7.00
9 Creamer	7.00
4 Cup	4.00
6 Mug, Hazel Atlas "Go-with"	5.00
3 Plate, 6⅞", salad	4.00
2 Plate, 8⅞", luncheon	5.00
1 Plate, 10½", sandwich	15.00

	All Colors
5 Saucer, 5⅝"	1.00
Sugar	7.00
Tidbit, 3-tier	35.00
Tumbler, 5 oz., juice (Hocking)	7.00
Tumbler, 6", 16 oz. (Hocking)	8.00
Tumbler, 6¼", 20 oz. (Hocking)	10.00
10 Tumbler Hazel Atlas "Go-with"	5.00

ROCK CRYSTAL, "EARLY AMERICAN ROCK CRYSTAL"

McKee Glass Company, 1920s and 1930s in color
pink, green, cobalt, red, yellow, amber, blue-green, crystal

	Crystal	Red		Crystal	Red
Bonbon, 7½", S.E.	22.00	60.00	Cake stand, 11", footed, 2¾" high...	35.00	125.00
Bowl, 4", 5", fruit, S.E.	16.00	32.00	Compote, 7"	30.00	95.00
Bowl, 5", finger bowl with 7"			Creamer, 9 oz., footed	20.00	65.00
plate, P.E.	35.00	70.00	Cruet & stopper, oil, 6 oz.	115.00	———
Bowl, 7", pickle or spoon tray	22.00	75.00	Cup, 7 oz.	15.00	70.00
Bowl, 7", 8", salad, S.E.	26.00	75.00	Goblet, 7½", 8 oz., low footed	18.00	57.50
Bowl, 9", 10½", salad, S.E.	35.00	125.00	Goblet, 11 oz., iced tea, low footed..	20.00	67.50
Bowl, 11½", 2-part, relish	35.00	83.00	Jelly, 5", footed, S.E.	30.00	52.50
Bowl, 12", oblong celery	28.00	95.00	Lamp, electric	295.00	695.00
Bowl, 12½", footed center bowl	65.00	295.00	2 Parfait, 3½ oz., low foot	20.00	75.00
Bowl, 13", roll tray	45.00	125.00	Pitcher, ½ gal., 7½" high	125.00	———
Bowl, 14", 6-part relish	50.00	———	Pitcher, lg., covered	175.00	895.00
Candelabra, 2-light, pr.	40.00	295.00	Plate, 6", bread & butter, S.E.	8.00	18.00
Candelabra, 3-light, pr.	65.00	395.00	5 Plate, 7", P.E.	10.00	22.00
Candlesticks, 5½", low, pr.	40.00	150.00	Plate, 7½", P.E. & S.E.	10.00	22.00
Candlesticks, 8½", tall, pr.	90.00	475.00			
Candy & cover, round	75.00	200.00			

S.E. — McKee designation for scalloped edge
P.E. — McKee designation for plain edge

Continued

157

ROCK CRYSTAL,
"EARLY AMERICAN ROCK CRYSTAL"

	Crystal	Red
Plate, 8½", P.E. & S.E.	15.00	35.00
Plate, 9", S.E.	18.00	55.00
Plate, 10½", S.E.	25.00	65.00
1 Plate, 10½", dinner, S.E. (lg. center design)	45.00	165.00
Plate, 11½", cake, S.E. (sm. center design)	18.00	55.00
Salt & pepper, 2 styles	90.00	——
Salt dip	60.00	——
Sandwich server, center hndl.	30.00	135.00
Saucer	6.00	16.00
Sherbet or egg, 3½ oz., footed	12.00	50.00
Stemware, 1 oz., footed cordial	18.00	45.00
Stemware, 2 oz., 3 oz., footed wines	20.00	43.00

	Crystal	Red
Stemware, 3½ oz., footed cocktail	12.00	45.00
Stemware, 6 oz., footed champagne	15.00	32.00
Stemware, 8 oz., lg. footed goblet	20.00	55.00
Sundae, 6 oz., low footed	10.00	32.00
Sugar, 10 oz., open, flat	15.00	——
Sugar, 10 oz., covered, footed	50.00	180.00
4 Syrup w/lid	225.00	895.00
Tumbler, whiskey, 2½ oz.	20.00	50.00
Tumbler, juice, 5 oz.	16.00	50.00
Tumbler, old fashioned, 5 oz.	20.00	60.00
3 Tumbler, 9 oz., concave or straight	22.00	50.00
Tumbler, 12 oz., concave or straight	28.00	75.00
Vase, 11", footed	75.00	225.00

S.E. — McKee designation for scalloped edge
P.E. — McKee designation for plain edge

"ROMANESQUE"
L.E. Smith Glass Co., Early 1930s
black, amber, crystal, pink, yellow, and green

	All Colors*
Bowl, 10", footed, 4¼" high	80.00
Bowl, 10½"	50.00
Cake plate, 11½" x 2¾"	45.00
Candlestick, 2½", pr.	30.00
Plate, 5½", octagonal	7.00
Plate, 7", octagonal	10.00
Plate, 8", octagonal	13.00

*Black or canary add 30%.

	All Colors*
Plate, 8", round	10.00
Plate, 10", octagonal	25.00
Plate, 10", octagonal, 2 hndl.	45.00
Sherbet, plain top	10.00
Sherbet, scalloped top	12.00
1 Tray, snack	15.00
Vase, 7½", fan	65.00

ROSE CAMEO
Belmont Tumbler Company, 1931
green

	Green		Green
5 Bowl, 4½", berry	15.00	4 Plate, 7", salad	12.00
6 Bowl, 5", cereal	20.00	2 Sherbet	12.00
3 Bowl, 6", straight side	30.00	1 Tumbler, 5", footed, 2 styles	20.00

ROSEMARY, "DUTCH ROSE"
Federal Glass Company, 1935 – 1937
pink, green, amber

	Amber	Green		Amber	Green
Bowl, 5", berry	5.00	9.00	1 Plate, dinner	9.00	15.00
Bowl, 5", cream soup	12.00	30.00	Plate, grill	10.00	20.00
Bowl, 6", cereal	20.00	40.00	Platter, 12", oval	15.00	27.00
Bowl, 10", oval vegetable	15.00	30.00	5 Saucer	2.00	5.00
Creamer, footed	8.00	12.50	Sugar, footed	8.00	12.50
Cup	6.00	9.50	2 Tumbler, 4¼", 9 oz.	24.00	40.00
Plate, 6¾", salad	6.00	8.50			

ROULETTE, "MANY WINDOWS"
Hocking Glass Company, 1935 – 1939
pink, green

	Pink	Green		Pink	Green
Bowl, 9", fruit	25.00	28.00	Sherbet	—	7.00
Cup	—	8.00	4 Tumbler, 3¼", juice, 5 oz.	28.00	30.00
1 Pitcher, 8", 64 oz.	45.00	45.00	3 Tumbler, 3¼", old fashioned, 7½ oz.	45.00	50.00
Plate, 6", sherbet	—	5.00	5 Tumbler, 4⅛", water, 9 oz.	30.00	30.00
Plate, 8½", luncheon	—	8.00	2 Tumbler, 5⅛", iced tea, 12 oz.	33.00	38.00
Plate, 12", sandwich	—	18.00	Tumbler, 5½", 10 oz., footed	—	38.00
Saucer	—	3.50	Whiskey, 2½", 1½ oz.	14.00	18.00

"ROUND ROBIN"
1927 – 1932
green, iridescent

	Green	Iridescent
7 Bowl, 4", berry	12.00	9.00
5 Cup, footed	6.00	7.00
3 Creamer, footed	12.50	9.00
8 Domino tray	125.00	—
Plate, 6", sherbet	3.50	2.50

	Green	Iridescent
Plate, 8", luncheon	8.00	4.00
Plate, 12", sandwich	12.00	12.00
4 Saucer	2.00	2.00
6 Sherbet	10.00	10.00
1 Sugar	12.50	9.00

ROXANA
Hazel Atlas Glass Company, 1932
yellow, white, crystal

	Yellow
Bowl, 4½" x 2⅜"	15.00
Bowl, 5", berry	18.00
6 Bowl, 6", cereal	20.00
1 Plate, 5½"	9.00

	Yellow
2 Plate, 6"	9.00
5 Sherbet, footed	10.00
3 Tumbler, 4", 9 oz.	20.00

ROYAL LACE
Hazel Atlas Glass Company, 1934 – 1941
pink, green, crystal, blue
See Reproduction Section, Page 213

	Pink	Blue		Pink	Blue
Bowl, 4¾", cream soup	30.00	42.00	Pitcher, 8", 86 oz.	135.00	—
Bowl, 5", berry	40.00	80.00	Pitcher, 8½", 96 oz.	150.00	495.00
Bowl, 10", round berry	35.00	80.00	Plate, 6", sherbet	10.00	17.00
Bowl, 10", 3-leg, straight edge	65.00	95.00	Plate, 8½", luncheon	20.00	42.00
Bowl, 10", 3-leg, rolled edge	135.00	750.00	Plate, 9⅞", dinner	30.00	48.00
Bowl, 10", 3-leg, ruffled edge	105.00	850.00	2 Plate, 9⅞", grill	25.00	40.00
Bowl, 11", oval vegetable	35.00	75.00	Platter, 13", oval	42.00	70.00
Butter dish & cover	225.00	695.00	Salt & pepper, pr.	65.00	320.00
Candlesticks, straight edge, pr.	75.00	165.00	5 Saucer	7.00	12.00
Candlesticks, rolled edge, pr.	160.00	550.00	Sherbet, footed	20.00	60.00
Candlesticks, ruffled edge, pr.	150.00	575.00	Sugar	18.00	37.50
*Cookie jar & cover	65.00	325.00	Sugar lid	60.00	195.00
Creamer, footed	20.00	55.00	Tumbler, 3½", 5 oz.	33.00	52.50
6 Cup	20.00	40.00	3 Tumbler, 4⅛", 9 oz.	25.00	50.00
Nut dish	595.00	1,695.00	Tumbler, 4⅞", 10 oz.	85.00	145.00
1 Pitcher, 48 oz., straight sides	100.00	175.00	4 Tumbler, 5⅜", 12 oz.	95.00	120.00
Pitcher, 8", 68 oz.	115.00	225.00			

* Beware of reproductions.

ROYAL RUBY
Anchor Hocking Glass Company, 1939 – 1960s
red

	Red
Ashtray, 4½", sq.	5.50
Bowl, 4¼", berry	5.50
Bowl, 5¼"	12.00
Bowl, 7½", soup	13.00
7 Bowl, 8", oval vegetable	20.00
Bowl, 8½", lg. berry	18.00
Bowl, 10", deep	40.00
Bowl, 11½", salad	30.00
Card holder or box w/lid	60.00
Creamer, flat	12.00
Creamer, footed	9.00
Cup (round or sq.)	6.00
Goblet, ball stem	12.00
Lamp	35.00
Pitcher, 24 oz., tilted or upright	35.00
Pitcher, 3 qt., tilted	50.00
Pitcher, 3 qt., upright	35.00
Plate, 6½", sherbet	4.00
Plate, 7", salad	5.00

	Red
Plate, 7¾", luncheon	6.00
Plate, 9" or 9¼", dinner	11.00
Plate, 13¾"	25.00
Punch bowl & stand	75.00
6 Punch cup	2.50
Saucer (round or sq.)	2.50
Sherbet, footed	8.00
Sugar, flat	12.00
Sugar, footed	8.00
Sugar lid	10.00
1 Tumbler, 2½", footed wine	14.00
Tumbler, 3½", cocktail	12.00
2 Tumbler, 5 oz., juice, 2 styles	7.00
3 Tumbler, 9 oz., water, ftd.	6.00
5 Tumbler, 13 oz., iced tea	12.50
Vase, 4", ball-shaped	6.00
4 Vase, 6½", bulbous, tall	9.00
Vases, several styles (sm.)	9.00
Vases, 9", 2 styles	17.50

"S" PATTERN, "STIPPLED ROSE BAND"
MacBeth-Evans Glass Company, 1930 – 1933
crystal, amber

	Crystal	Amber		Crystal	Amber
Bowl, 5½", cereal	5.00	9.00	Plate, 11", heavy cake	50.00	——
Bowl, 8½", lg. berry	15.00	20.00	Plate, 13", heavy cake	70.00	90.00
Creamer, thick or thin	6.00	7.00	Saucer	2.00	2.50
Cup, thick or thin	3.50	4.50	2 Sherbet, low footed	4.50	8.00
Pitcher, 80 oz.	65.00	160.00	4 Sugar, thick & thin	6.00	6.50
Plate, 6", sherbet	2.50	3.00	Tumbler, 3½", 5 oz.	6.00	8.00
Plate, 8", luncheon	7.00	6.00	Tumbler, 4", 9 oz.	10.00	12.00
Plate, 9¼", dinner	——	10.00	Tumbler, 4¼", 10 oz.	12.00	12.00
Plate, grill	6.00	9.00	Tumbler, 5", 12 oz.	14.00	16.00

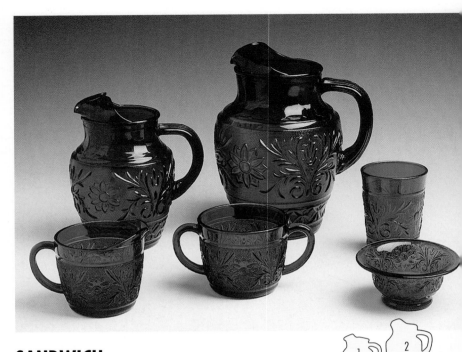

SANDWICH

Hocking Glass Company, 1939 – 1964
crystal, 1930 – 1960s; amber (desert gold),
1960s; pink and ruby red, 1939 – 1940; forest green, 1950 – 1960s; white (opaque),1950s

See Reproduction Section, Page 214

	Crystal	Green
Bowl, 4⅞", berry	5.00	6.00
Bowl, 6½", smooth or scalloped	8.00	60.00
Bowl, 6¾", cereal	42.00	—
Bowl, 7", salad	7.00	95.00
Bowl, 8", smooth or scalloped	12.00	110.00
Bowl, 8¼", oval	8.00	—
Butter dish, low	45.00	—
Cookie jar & cover	40.00	—
4 Creamer	6.00	30.00
Cup, tea or coffee	2.50	18.00
6 Custard cup	3.00	3.00
Custard cup liner	20.00	1.50
1 Pitcher, 6", juice	50.00	195.00
2 Pitcher, ½ gal., ice lip	80.00	495.00

* No lid

	Crystal	Green
Plate, 7", dessert	10.00	—
Plate, 8"	7.00	—
Plate, 9", dinner	15.00	125.00
Plate, 9" indent for punch cup	5.00	—
Plate, 12", sandwich	35.00	—
Punch bowl, 9¾"	20.00	—
Punch stand	30.00	—
Punch cup	2.25	—
Saucer	1.50	12.00
Sherbet, footed	7.00	—
5 Sugar & cover	22.00	25.00
Tumbler, 3 oz., juice	18.00	—
Tumbler, 5 oz., juice	6.00	4.00
3 Tumbler, 9 oz., water	8.00	5.00
Tumbler, 9 oz., footed	28.00	

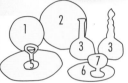

SANDWICH
Indiana Glass Company, 1920 – 1970s
crystal, amber, pink, red, teal blue, light green
See Reproduction Section, Page 215

	Crystal	Pink
Ashtray set (club, spade, heart,		
diamond shapes), each	3.00	——
Bowl, 4¼", berry	3.50	——
Bowl, 6"	4.00	——
Bowl, 6", 6 sides	5.00	——
Bowl, 8½"	11.00	——
Bowl, 9", console	16.00	40.00
Bowl, 11½", console	20.00	50.00
Butter dish & cover, domed	20.00	——
Candlesticks, 3½", pr.	17.50	45.00
Candlesticks, 7", pr.	25.00	——
Creamer, diamond	4.00	——
Creamer, flat	9.00	45.00
Cruet, 6½", & stopper	22.00	——
Cup	3.00	——
Creamer & sugar on		
diamond-shaped tray	16.00	——
3 Decanter & stopper	22.00	125.00

	Crystal	Pink
Goblet, 9 oz.	13.00	——
Pitcher, 68 oz.	25.00	——
Plate, 6", sherbet	3.00	——
1 Plate, 7", bread & butter	4.00	——
6 Plate, 8", oval, indent for sherbet	5.00	——
Plate, 8⅜", luncheon	5.00	——
2 Plate, 10½", dinner	8.00	18.00
Plate, 13", sandwich	13.00	25.00
5 Sandwich server, center hndl.	16.00	27.50
Saucer	2.00	——
7 Sherbet	5.00	15.00
Sugar, diamond	5.00	——
Sugar, flat	9.00	45.00
Tumbler, 3 oz., footed cocktail	7.50	——
Tumbler, 8 oz., footed water	9.00	——
Tumbler, 12 oz., footed iced tea	10.00	——
Wine, 3", 4 oz.	6.00	22.50

SHARON, "CABBAGE ROSE"
Federal Glass Company, 1935 – 1939
pink, green, amber, crystal
See Reproduction Section, Page 216 – 218

	Amber	Pink		Amber	Pink
6 Bowl, 5", berry	7.00	10.00	Plate, 6", bread & butter	2.00	4.00
Bowl, 5", cream soup	20.00	40.00	Plate, 7½", salad	12.00	18.00
3 Bowl, 6", cereal	17.50	22.00	1 Plate, 9½", dinner	9.00	15.00
Bowl, 7½", flat soup, 2" deep	40.00	48.00	Platter, 12½", oval	14.00	25.00
Bowl, 8½", lg. berry	5.00	25.00	Salt & pepper, pr.	33.00	45.00
Bowl, 9½", oval vegetable	15.00	25.00	5 Saucer	3.00	5.00
Bowl, 10½", fruit	20.00	33.00	Sherbet, footed	8.00	12.00
Butter dish & cover	42.00	52.00	Sugar	8.00	10.00
Cake plate, footed, 11½"	25.00	35.00	Sugar lid	20.00	30.00
Candy jar & cover	45.00	48.00	Tumbler, 4⅛", 9 oz.,		
Cheese dish & cover	210.00	1,650.00	thin	25.00	38.00
Creamer, footed	10.00	12.50	2 thick	25.00	42.00
4 Cup	6.00	8.00	Tumbler, 5¼", 12 oz.,		
Jam dish, 7½"	28.00	195.00	thin	50.00	50.00
Pitcher, 80 oz., with or without			thick	60.00	90.00
ice lip	135.00	180.00	Tumbler, 6½", footed, 15 oz.	80.00	45.00

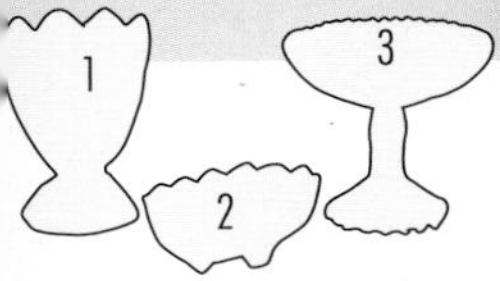

SHELL PINK MILK GLASS
Jeannette Glass Co., 1957 – 1959

Ashtray, butterfly shape	20.00
Base, for lazy Susan, with ball bearings	160.00
Bowl, 6½", wedding, with cover	20.00
Bowl, 8", pheasant, footed	35.00
Bowl, 8", wedding, with cover	25.00
Bowl, 9", footed, fruit stand, Floragold	30.00
Bowl, 10", Florentine, footed	30.00
Bowl, 10½", footed, Holiday	45.00
Bowl, 10⅞", 4-footed, Lombardi, designed center	40.00
Bowl, 10⅞", 4-footed, Lombardi, plain center	25.00
Bowl, 17½", gondola fruit	40.00
Cake plate, anniversary	275.00
Cake stand, 10", harp	45.00
Candle holder, 2-light, pr.	50.00
Candle holder, eagle, 3-footed, pr.	70.00
Candy dish with cover, 6½" high, sq.	30.00
Candy dish, 4-footed, 5¼", floragold	20.00
Candy jar, 5½", 4-footed, with cover, grapes	20.00
Celery and relish, 12½", 3-part	40.00
Cigarette box, butterfly finial	210.00
Compote, 6", Windsor	20.00
Cookie jar with cover, 6½" high	150.00
Creamer, Baltimore pear design	15.00
Honey jar, beehive shape, notched cover	50.00
"Napco" #2249, cross hatch design pot	15.00

"Napco" #2250, footed bowl with berries	15.00
"Napco" #2255, footed bowl with sawtooth top	25.00
"Napco" #2256, sq. comport	12.50
"National" candy bottom	10.00
Pitcher, 24 oz., footed, thumbprint	25.00
Powder jar, 4¾", with cover	40.00
Punch base, 3½" tall	30.00
Punch bowl, 7½ qt.	110.00
Punch cup, 5 oz. (also fits snack tray)	4.00
Punch ladle, pink plastic	20.00
Punch set, 15 pc. (bowl, base, 12 cups, ladle)	210.00
Relish, 12", 4-part, octagonal, vineyard design	40.00
Stem, 5 oz., sherbet, Thumbprint	9.00
Stem, 8 oz., water goblet, Thumbprint	12.50
Sugar cover	15.00
Sugar, footed, Baltimore pear design	12.00
Tray, 7¾" x 10", snack with cup indent	8.00
Tray, 12½" x 9¾", 2 hndl., harp	60.00
Tray, 13½", lazy Susan, 5-part	60.00
Tray, 15¾", 5-part, 2 hndl.	75.00
Tray, 16½", 6-part, Venetian	35.00
Tray, Lazy Susan complete with base	225.00
Tumbler, 5 oz., juice, footed, thumbprint	8.00
Vase, 5", Cornucopia	15.00
Vase, 7"	35.00
Vase, 9", heavy bottom	165.00

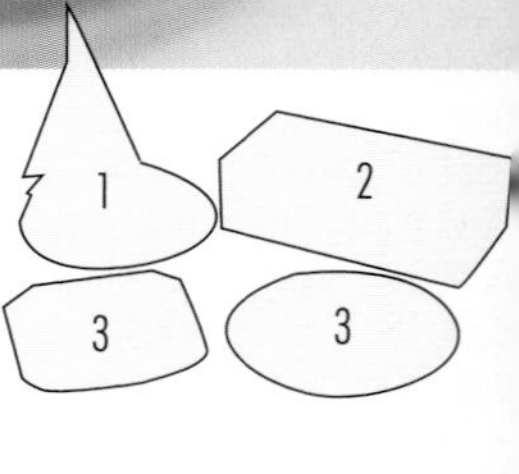

"SHIPS" or "SAILBOAT," also known as "SPORTSMAN SERIES"

Hazel Atlas Glass Co., Late 1930s

cobalt blue with white, yellow, and red decoration, crystal with blue

All pieces shown are not verified Hazel-Atlas but are collected as "Go-withs."

		Blue/White
3	*Ashtray, sq. or rd.	20.00 – 30.00
2	*Cigarette box	100.00 – 110.00
	Cup (plain) "Moderntone"	12.00
	Cocktail mixer with stirrer	35.00
	Cocktail shaker	40.00
	Ice bowl	40.00
1	*Metal ship ashtray	50.00 – 60.00
	Pitcher without lip, 82 oz.	70.00
	Pitcher with lip, 86 oz.	75.00
	Plate, 5⅞", sherbet	35.00
	Plate, 8", salad	35.00
	Plate, 9", dinner	50.00

	Blue/Whi
Saucer	22.00
Tumbler, 2 oz., 2¼", Shot Glass	235.00
Tumbler, 3½", whiskey	25.00
Tumbler, 4 oz., heavy bottom	25.00
Tumbler, 4 oz., 3¼", heavy bottom	25.00
Tumbler, 5 oz., 3¾", juice	16.00*
Tumbler, 6 oz., roly poly	12.50
Tumbler, 8 oz., 3⅜", old fashioned	20.00
Tumbler, 9 oz., 3¾", straight, water	16.00
Tumbler, 9 oz., 4⅝", water	15.00*
Tumbler, 101/2 oz., 47/8", iced tea	16.00
Tumbler, 12 oz., iced tea	25.00*

*"Go-with"

**Crystal 50% less

SIERRA, "PINWHEEL"
Jeannette Glass Company, 1931 – 1933
pink, green

	Pink	Green
Bowl, 5½", cereal	15.00	16.00
Bowl, 8½", lg. berry	35.00	40.00
Bowl, 9½", oval vegetable	100.00	160.00
Butter dish & cover	75.00	80.00
Creamer	20.00	25.00
Cup	15.00	15.00
Pitcher, 6½", 32 oz.	140.00	175.00
Plate, 9", dinner	22.00	28.00

	Pink	Green
Platter, 11", oval	55.00	75.00
Salt & pepper, pr.	45.00	45.00
5 Saucer	9.00	9.00
Serving tray, 2 hndl.	25.00	20.00
Sugar	25.00	30.00
Sugar cover	20.00	20.00
1 Tumbler, 4½", 9 oz., footed	75.00	100.00

SPIRAL
Hocking Glass Company, 1928 – 1930
green, crystal

	Green
Bowl, 4¾", berry	8.00
Bowl, 7", mixing	15.00
Bowl, 8", lg. berry	12.50
4 Creamer, flat or footed	10.00
Cup	7.00
Ice or butter tub	30.00
Pitcher, 7⅜", 58 oz.	40.00
2 Plate, 6", sherbet	3.00
1 Plate, 8", luncheon	4.00
Platter	35.00

	Green
6 Preserve & cover	40.0
Salt & pepper, pr.	35.0
Sandwich server, center hndl.	25.0
Saucer	2.0
Sherbet	5.0
3 Sugar, flat or footed	10.0
Tumbler, 3", juice, 5 oz.	4.5
Tumbler, 5", water, 9 oz.	10.0
Tumbler, 5⅞", footed	18.0
5 Vase, 5¾", footed	75.0

STAR
Federal Glass Company, 1950s
amber, crystal and crystal with gold trim

	Crystal	Yellow		Crystal	Yellow
Bowl, 4⅝", dessert	4.00	7.00	2 Plate, 9⅜", dinner	5.00	10.00
Bowl, 8⅜", vegetable	10.00	20.00	Plate, 11¾", sandwich	12.00	18.00
Butter dish, round	90.00	——	Saucer	2.00	4.00
5 Creamer	6.00	10.00	4 Sugar	5.00	6.00
Cup	4.00	10.00	Sugar lid	7.00	14.00
3 Pitcher, 5¾", 36 oz., juice	9.00	——	Tumbler, 2¼", 1½ oz., whiskey	3.00	——
1 Pitcher, 7", 60 oz.	10.00	——	Tumbler, 3⅜", 4½ oz., juice	4.00	10.00
Pitcher, 9¼", 85 oz., ice lip	12.00	——	Tumbler, 3⅞", 9 oz., water	5.00	12.00
Plate, 6³⁄₁₆", salad	3.00	6.00	Tumbler, 5⅛", 12 oz., iced tea	7.00	16.00

STARLIGHT
Hazel Atlas Glass Company, 1938 – 1940
pink, white, crystal, cobalt blue

	Crystal	Pink		Crystal	Pink
5 Bowl, 5½", cereal, closed hndl.	9.00	12.00	1 Plate, 9", dinner	8.00	——
Bowl, 8½", closed hndl.	10.00	20.00	Plate, 13", sandwich	12.00	18.00
Bowl, 11½", salad	25.00	——	Relish dish	12.00	——
Creamer, oval	6.00	——	Salt & pepper, pr.	20.00	——
4 Cup	5.00	——	3 Saucer	2.00	——
2 Plate, 6", bread & butter	2.00	——	Sherbet	12.00	——
Plate, 8½", luncheon	4.00	——	Sugar, oval	6.00	——

STARS & STRIPES
Anchor Hocking Glass Co., 1942
crystal

	Crystal
Plate, 8"	12.00
Sherbet	10.00

	Crystal
1 Tumbler, 5", 10 oz.	50.00

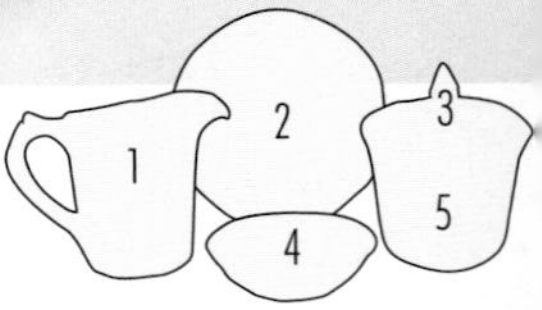

STRAWBERRY
U.S. Glass Company, 1928 – 1931
pink, green, iridescent

	Pink or Green
4 Bowl, 4", berry	12.00
Bowl, 6¼", 2" deep	150.00
Bowl, 7½", deep berry	25.00
Butter dish & cover	155.00
Compote, 5¾"	32.00
Creamer, sm.	20.00
1 Creamer, lg., 4⅝"	40.00
Olive dish, 5", 1 hndl.	22.00
Pickle dish	20.00
Pitcher, 7¾"	225.00
2 Plate, 6", sherbet	12.00
Plate, 7½", salad	18.00
Sherbet	10.00
Sugar, sm., open	22.00
5 Sugar, lg.	40.00
3 Sugar cover	60.00
Tumbler, 3⅝", 9 oz.	35.00

SUNBURST
Jeannette Glass Company, Late 1920s

3 Bowl, 4¾", berry 6.00
　Bowl, 8½", berry 15.00
　Bowl, 10¾" 18.00
　Candlesticks, double, pr. 20.00
5 Creamer, footed 6.00
　Cup 6.00
　Plate, 5½" 5.00
　Plate, 9¼", dinner.. 12.00

1 Plate, 11¾", sandwich.. 20.00
6 Relish, 2-part 8.00
　Saucer.. 2.00
4 Sherbet.. 12.00
2 Sugar 6.00
　Tumbler, 4", 9 oz., flat... 40.00
　Tray, small, oval 9.00

SUNFLOWER
Jeannette Glass Company, Late 1920s
pink, green, ultramarine

	Pink	Green
Ashtray, 5", center design only	9.00	11.00
Cake plate, 10", 3 legs	15.00	15.00
Creamer	28.00	28.00
Cup	18.00	20.00
2 Plate, 8", luncheon	25.00	———

	Pink	Green
1 Plate, 9", dinner	25.00	25.00
Saucer	10.00	10.00
Sugar	25.00	25.00
Trivet, 7", 3 legs, turned-up edge	395.00	395.00
Tumbler, 4¾", 8 oz., footed	38.00	38.00

SWIRL, "PETAL SWIRL"
Jeannette Glass Company, 1937 – 1938
pink, ultramarine, delphite

	Pink	Ultra-marine		Pink	Ultra-marine
Bowl, 5¼", cereal	13.00	16.00	Plate, 8", salad	10.00	15.00
Bowl, 9", salad	26.00	28.00	Plate, 9¼", dinner	18.00	22.00
Bowl, 10", footed, closed hndl.	35.00	32.00	Plate, 12½", sandwich	22.00	28.00
Bowl, 10½", console, footed	20.00	30.00	Salt & pepper, pr.	——	50.00
Butter dish	190.00	350.00	2 Saucer	3.00	4.00
Candleholders, double branch, pr.	90.00	60.00	Sherbet, low footed	16.00	23.00
Candy dish, open, 3 legs	14.00	16.00	Soup, tab hndl. (lug)	45.00	55.00
Candy dish with cover	110.00	165.00	Sugar, footed	11.00	15.00
Coaster, 1" x 3¼"	15.00	20.00	Tumbler, 4", 9 oz.	20.00	33.00
Creamer, footed	11.00	15.00	Tumbler, 5⅛", 13 oz.	60.00	135.00
1 Cup	11.00	15.00	Tumbler, 9 oz., footed	22.00	40.00
Pitcher, 48 oz., footed	——	2,000.00	Vase, 6½", footed	25.00	——
Plate, 6½", sherbet	7.00	7.00	Vase, 8½", footed	——	27.50
Plate, 7¼"	11.00	16.00			

TEA ROOM
Indiana Glass Company, 1926 – 1931
green, pink, crystal, amber

	Green	Pink		Green	Pink
Bowl, finger	90.00	85.00	1 Plate, 8¼", luncheon	45.00	40.00
Bowl, 7½", banana split, ftd.	165.00	200.00	Plate, 10½", 2 hndl.	65.00	60.00
3 Bowl, 7½", banana split, flat	100.00	125.00	Relish, divided	27.00	30.00
Bowl, 8½", celery	32.00	36.00	2 Salt & pepper, pr.	110.00	100.00
Bowl, 8¾", deep salad	100.00	125.00	4 Saucer	30.00	30.00
Bowl, 9½", oval vegetable	55.00	55.00	Sherbet, 3 styles	35.00	30.00
Candlestick, low, pr.	85.00	65.00	Sugar, 4"	22.00	20.00
Creamer, 4"	22.00	22.00	Sugar, flat with cover	225.00	200.00
Creamer & sugar on tray, 3½"	90.00	90.00	Sundae, footed, ruffled	135.00	175.00
5 Cup	75.00	65.00	Tumbler, 8½ oz., flat	160.00	150.00
Goblet, 9 oz.	85.00	75.00	Tumbler, 6 oz., footed	40.00	35.00
Ice bucket	95.00	90.00	6 Tumbler, 8 oz., footed	35.00	35.00
Lamp, electric	155.00	140.00	Tumbler, 11 oz., footed	55.00	55.00
Mustard, covered	210.00	175.00	Tumbler, 12 oz., footed	75.00	80.00
Parfait	165.00	115.00	Vase, 9½"	130.00	—
Pitcher, 64 oz.	185.00	150.00	Vase, 11", ruffled edge	300.00	300.00
Plate, 6½", sherbet	25.00	25.00	Vase, 11", straight	160.00	165.00

THISTLE
MacBeth-Evans, 1929 – 1930
pink, green, crystal

	Pink	Green		Pink	Green
2 Bowl, 5½", cereal	35.00	38.00	Plate, 10¼", grill	30.00	35.00
Bowl, 10¼", lg. fruit	595.00	395.00	1 Plate, 13", cake, heavy	210.00	235.00
3 Cup, thin	28.00	30.00	4 Saucer	10.00	12.00
Plate, 8", luncheon	17.00	18.00			

THOUSAND LINE, "STARS & BARS," "RAINBOW STARS"

Anchor Hocking Glass Co., 1941 – 1960s
crystal, satinized green

	Crystal
Bowl, 6", hndl.	10.00
Bowl, 7½" deep	10.00
Bowl, 8", vegetable	12.00
Bowl, 10½", salad, flat base, 7" center	25.00
Bowl, 10⅞", vegetable, rim base, 5½" center	15.00
3 Candle, 4"	4.00
4 Candy with lid	20.00
Creamer, 2½"	4.00
Fork	7.50

	Crystal
Plate, 8", lunch	11.00
Relish, 12", 6-part	15.00
2 Relish, 3-part, round	8.00
1 Relish, 10", 2 hndl., oval	7.00
Spoon	7.50
Sugar, 2½"	4.00
Tray, 12½", sandwich	14.00
Vase, bud	13.00

TULIP
Dell Glass Company, early 1930s
amethyst, blue, green, crystal

	Amethyst/Blue	Green/Crystal		Amethyst/Blue	Green/Crystal
Bowl, oval, oblong, 13¼"	90.00	75.00	Plate, 6"	9.00	8.00
Candleholder, 3¾", pr.			Plate, 7¼"	15.00	12.00
(like sherbet)	70.00	60.00	1 Plate, 10"	35.00	32.00
Candy with lid	225.00	185.00	5 Saucer	6.00	5.00
2 Creamer	20.00	20.00	Sherbet, 3¾", flat	20.00	18.00
4 Cup	16.00	14.00	3 Sugar	20.00	20.00
Decanter with stopper	495.00	—	Tumbler, juice	30.00	20.00
Ice tub, 4⅞" wide, 3" deep	55.00	50.00	Tumbler, whiskey	32.00	23.00

185

TWISTED OPTIC
Imperial Glass Company, 1927 – 1930
pink, green, amber, crystal, yellow

	Pink or Green
Basket	60.00
Bowl, 5", cereal	9.00
Bowl, 7", salad or soup	15.00
Candlestick, 3", pr.	40.00
1 Candy jar & cover	40.00
Creamer	10.00
3 Cup	7.00
Pitcher, 64 oz.	45.00
Plate, 6", sherbet	3.00
Plate, 7", salad	4.00

	Pink or Green
Plate, 7½" x 9", oval w/ indent	7.00
Plate, 8", luncheon	7.00
Preserve (same as candy but with slot in lid)	30.00
Sandwich server, center hndl.	20.00
Sandwich server, 2 hndl., flat	12.00
2 Saucer	2.00
Sherbet	6.00
Sugar	10.00
Tumbler, 4½", 9 oz.	6.00
Tumbler, 5¼", 12 oz.	9.00

U.S. SWIRL
U.S. Glass Company, late 1920s
pink, green

	Green	Pink
Bowl, 4⅜", berry	5.00	6.00
Bowl, 5½", 1 hndl.	9.00	10.00
Bowl, 7⅛", lg. berry	15.00	16.00
Bowl, 8¼", oval	60.00	55.00
Butter & cover	100.00	100.00
Butter bottom	80.00	80.00
Butter top	20.00	20.00
Candy, ftd., 2 hndl.	35.00	30.00
Candy with cover, 2 hndl.	30.00	35.00
Comport, 5¼"	35.00	30.00

	Green	Pink
Creamer	25.00	25.00
6 Pickle dish, 8¼", oval	30.00	30.00
2 Pitcher, 8", 48 oz.	75.00	75.00
Plate, 6⅛", sherbet	2.50	2.50
Plate, 7⅞", salad	5.00	6.00
Salt & pepper, pr.	75.00	75.00
Sherbet, 3¼"	4.00	5.00
Sugar with lid	40.00	40.00
5 Tumbler, 4⅝", 12 oz.	15.00	16.00
Vase, 6½"	32.00	28.00

"VICTORY"
Diamond Glassware Company, 1929 – 1932
amber, green, pink, cobalt blue

	Pink	Blue
Bonbon, 7"	10.00	18.00
5 Bowl, 6½", cereal	12.00	35.00
Bowl, 8½", flat soup	18.00	60.00
Bowl, 9", oval vegetable	35.00	100.00
Bowl, 11", rolled edge	25.00	45.00
Bowl, 12", console	35.00	65.00
Bowl, 12½", flat edge	30.00	70.00
Candlestick, 3", pr.	35.00	120.00
Cheese & cracker set, 12" indented plate & compote	35.00	——
1 Comport, 6" tall, 6¾" diameter	15.00	——
4 Creamer	12.00	35.00
7 Cup	12.00	25.00

	Pink	Bl
Goblet, 5", 7 oz	22.00	70.0
Gravy boat & platter	200.00	250.0
Mayonnaise set: 3½" tall, 5½" across, 8½" indented plate with ladle	38.00	90.0
Plate, 6", bread & butter	4.00	12.
Plate, 7", salad	6.00	15.
2 Plate, 8", luncheon	7.00	24.
Plate, 9", dinner	18.00	40.
Platter, 12"	26.00	75.
Sandwich server, center hndl.	30.00	60.
6 Saucer	3.00	7.
Sherbet, footed	12.00	24.
3 Sugar	12.00	35.

VITROCK ("FLOWER RIM")
Anchor Hocking Glass Company, 1934 – late 1930s
white

	White			White
Bowl, 4", berry	3.00	2	Plate, 7¼", salad	3.00
Bowl, 5½", cream soup	12.00	1	Plate, 8¾", luncheon	4.00
Bowl, 6", fruit	5.00		Plate, 9", soup	26.00
Bowl, 7½", cereal	7.00		Plate, 10", dinner	7.00
Bowl, vegetable	12.00		Platter, 11½"	22.00
Creamer, oval	5.00	6	Saucer	1.00
Cup	5.00	4	Sugar, oval	5.00

WAKEFIELD
Line #1932, Westmoreland Glass Co., circa 1932;
Waterford, 1950s – 1960s;
Wakefield with red trim , circa 1970s and beyond
crystal, crystal with red

	Crystal w/ Red Stain
Basket, 6"	70.00
Bonbon, 6", crimped, metal hndl.	35.00
Bowl, 5", heart, with hndl.	28.00
Bowl, 5", nappy, round, with hndl.	25.00
Bowl, 6", cupped	23.00
Bowl, 6", heart, with handle	40.00
Bowl, 8", heart, with handle	80.00
Bowl, 10½", bell, footed	75.00
Bowl, 11", flat, lipped	65.00
Bowl, 12", flat, crimped	85.00
Bowl, 12", footed, crimped	90.00
Bowl, 12", footed, straight edge	70.00
Bowl, 13", shallow server	70.00
Cake stand, 12", low foot	85.00
Candlestick, 6"	60.00
Compote, 5", low foot	30.00
Compote, 5", low foot, crimped	35.00
Compote, 5½", high foot, mint	32.00

	Crystal w/ Red Sta.
Compote, 7", high foot	50.0
Compote, 7", high foot, crimped	55.0
Compote, 12", low foot, fruit	85.0
Creamer, footed	60.0
Fairy lamp, 2-pc.	65.0
Plate, 6"	12.5
Plate, 8½", luncheon	22.5
Plate, 10", dinner	65.0
Plate, 14", torte	75.0
Stem, 1 oz., cordial	50.0
Stem, 2 oz., wine	32.0
Stem, 6 oz., sherbet	23.0
Stem, 10 oz., water	32.0
Sugar	60.0
Sweetmeat, crimped top	35.0
Tidbit tray, ruffled, metal hndl.	35.0
Tumbler, 12 oz., footed tea	27.0
Vase, crimped top	65.0

WATERFORD, "WAFFLE"
Hocking Glass Company, 1938 – 1944
crystal, pink

	Crystal	Pink		Crystal	Pink
Ashtray	7.50	—	Plate, 6", sherbet	3.00	7.00
Bowl, 4¾", berry	6.50	18.00	5 Plate, 7⅛", salad	6.00	15.00
2 Bowl, 5½", cereal	17.00	35.00	1 Plate, 9⅝", dinner	10.00	24.00
Bowl, 8¼", lg. berry	13.00	28.00	Plate, 10¼", hndl. cake	9.00	18.00
Butter dish & cover	20.00	225.00	Plate, 13¾", sandwich	12.00	38.00
Coaster, 4"	3.00	—	Salt & pepper, 2 types	6.00	—
Creamer, oval	5.00	12.00	4 Saucer	1.00	5.00
6 Cup	5.00	15.00	Sherbet, footed	4.00	20.00
Goblet, 5¼", 5⅝"	15.00	—	Sugar	5.00	12.00
Pitcher, juice, 24 oz., tilted	22.00	—	Sugar cover, oval	12.00	33.00
Pitcher, 80 oz., ice lip, tilted	36.00	175.00	3 Tumbler, 4⅞", 10 oz., footed	11.00	28.00

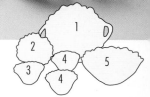

WILD ROSE WITH LEAVES & BERRIES
Indiana Glass Co., Early 1950s – 1980s

crystal, crystal satinized, iridescent, milk Glass, multicolored blue, green, pink, and yellow; satinized green, pink, and yellow; sprayed green, lavender, and pink

	Crystal or Sprayed	Multicolored		Crystal or Sprayed	Multicolored
Bowl, hndl. sauce	4.00	15.00	Relish, hndl.	7.00	30.00
5 Bowl, lg. vegetable	10.00	50.00	Relish, 2-part, hndl.	7.00	30.00
3 Candle	5.00	25.00	4 Sherbet	4.00	15.00
2 Plate, sherbet	2.00	10.00	1 Tray, 2 hndl.	12.00	50.00

WINDSOR, "WINDSOR DIAMOND"
Jeannette Glass Company, 1932 – 1946
pink, green, crystal

	Crystal	Pink		Crystal	Pink
Ashtray, 5¾"	12.00	35.00	Plate, 6", sherbet	2.50	5.00
Bowl, 4¾", berry	4.00	12.00	Plate, 7", salad	5.00	20.00
Bowl, 5", cream soup	7.00	25.00	Plate, 9", dinner	8.00	22.00
Bowl, 5⅛", 5⅜", cereals	8.00	20.00	Plate, 10¼", sandwich, hndl.	7.00	25.00
Bowl, 7⅛", 3 legs	9.00	28.00	Plate, 13⅝", chop	18.00	36.00
Bowl, 8½", lg. berry	10.00	25.00	Platter, 11½", oval	14.00	25.00
Bowl, 9½", oval vegetable	9.00	22.00	Relish platter, 11½", divided	15.00	250.00
Bowl, 12½", fruit console	30.00	130.00	Salt & pepper, pr.	20.00	40.00
Bowl, 7" x 11¾", boat shape	18.00	20.00	Saucer	2.00	5.00
Butter dish	25.00	65.00	Sherbet, footed	3.50	13.00
Cake plate, 10¾", footed	9.00	25.00	2 Sugar & cover	12.00	30.00
Candlesticks, 3", pr.	25.00	110.00	Tray, 4" sq.	5.00	10.00
Candy jar & cover	20.00	——	Tray, 4⅛" x 9"	5.00	10.00
Coaster, 3¼"	6.00	15.00	Tray, 8½" x 9¾"	6.50	24.00
Compote	10.00	——	1 Tray, 8½" x 9¾", 3 part	20.00	90.00
Creamer	5.00	14.00	Tumbler, 3¼", 5 oz.	12.00	15.00
Cup	4.00	10.00	Tumbler, 4", 9 oz.	7.00	13.00
Pitcher, 4½", 16 oz.	25.00	195.00	Tumbler, 5", 12 oz.	10.00	24.00
Pitcher, 6¾", 52 oz.	25.00	35.00	Tumbler, 7¼", footed	15.00	——

YORKTOWN
Federal Glass Co., mid-1950s
yellow, crystal, white, iridized, and smoke

	Crystal/Yellow
Bowl, 5½", berry, #2905	4.00
Bowl, 9½", lg. berry, #2906	11.00
Bowl, 10", footed, fruit, #2902	20.00
Celery tray, 10", #2907	12.00
Creamer, #2908	4.00
Cup, #2910	3.00
Cup, snack/punch, 6 oz.	1.50
Mug, 5¹⁄₁₆"	17.50
Plate, 8¼", #2903	4.00
Plate, 8½" x 6¾", snack with indent	2.00

	Crystal/Yellow
Plate, 11½", #2904	9.00
Punch set, 7 qt., base, 12 cups	30.00
Saucer, #2911	.50
Sherbet, 2½", 7 oz., #1744	3.00
Sugar with lid, #2909	8.00
Tumbler, 3⅞", 6 oz., juice, #1741	4.00
Tumbler, 4¾", 10 oz., water, #1742	5.00
Tumbler, 5¼", 13 oz., iced tea, #1743	9.00
Vase, 8"	16.00

Reproductions

As the popularity of any item in the collecting field grows, there is always someone or some company that will take advantage of the collector. This section will show you the reproductions in Depression glass through May 2006.

Know your glassware and your dealer before spending your hard-earned cash for it; also, be wary of deals that seem too good to be true.

The items pictured in this section have all been reproduced since 1973 either by the original glass companies themselves or by private individuals.

Items introduced by companies are usually available in the local dish barns or merchant stores. Those privately manufactured are found at flea markets, local antique or junk shops, and auctions.

Some of the glass is marketed through private sales or parties much like the Tupperware parties. In these, the buyer is treated to "exclusive lines" of glassware.

Our personal feeling is that as long as people buy these reproductions, re-issues, new products made to look old, or what have you, then they will continue to be made either privately or by the companies themselves. We feel also that buying a collectible is an investment, but buying a reproduction is merely speculation. These latter products appeal to us as much as swamp land in Florida.

What can we do? First, we can educate ourselves; secondly, we can refrain from buying the newer glass. Barring that, we who know the reproductions can label them as such when the opportunity arises.

"NEW ADAM"
Privately produced out of Korea through St. Louis Importing Company

The new Adam butter is no longer being offered at $7.00 wholesale. Identification of the new is easy. The following only applies to butter dishes and cannot be used to determine authenticity of other items in this pattern.
Use these tell-tale signs only for the butter dish.

Top: Notice the veins in the leaves.
New: Large leaf veins do not join or touch in center of leaf.
Old: Large leaf veins all touch or join center vein on the old.

A further note in the original Adam butter dish — the veins of all the leaves at the center of the design are very clear-cut and precisely molded, whereas in the new, these center leaf veins are very indistinct and almost invisible in open leaf of the center design.

Bottom: Place butter dish bottom upside down for observation.
New: Four "arrowhead-like" points line up in the northwest, northeast, southeast, and southwest directions.
Old: Four "arrowhead-like" points line up in north, east, south, and west directions.

There are very bad mold lines and very glossy light pink color on the new butter dishes I have examined, but these could be improved.

NEW "AVOCADO"
Indiana Glass Company, Tiara Exclusives Line, 1974...1990s
pink, frosted pink, yellow, blue, red, amethyst, dark green, frost green

The company only overlapped the original glass colors in pink. Green has been made, but note that it's a darker shade than the original green. A few additional items were made in yellow, but that was never a problem for collectors since yellow was not an original color. The original pink color is lighter in shade than this newer pink which has a slight orange tint.

Some of these sets, such as red, were made in limited editions as a selling point with buyers who are hopeful that someday they may be more valuable. Perhaps they shall; but we personally feel it will take many years for these to command more than their original value.

NEW "CHERRY BLOSSOM"
Privately Produced In 1973...
pink, green, blue, delphite, red, cobalt blue, various iridized colors

In 1973 the Depression glass world was stunned with the appearance of a child's butter dish and some odd-looking child's cups — odd because no child's butter dish was made originally and because in the bottoms of the cups, the cherry design was hanging upside-down. Since then, the upside-down design has been rectified and some saucers and plates have appeared. However, all these reproductions are easily spotted. **The child's creamer and sugar have not been reproduced!**

In 1977 butter dishes and shakers appeared. Some shakers in pink and green were dated '77; other pink, green, and delphite shakers appeared non-dated. These shakers are readily recognizable by the almost squared protrusions around the top edge of the shakers. We call them helicopter blades. On the original shakers these protrusions are more rounded and they extend only slightly outward from the top. If you wish to carry your examinations further than that, the design on the shakers is weaker in spots on the newer versions. Only **two** original pairs of pink shakers have ever been found!

The butter dishes pose a bit more problem in distinguishing old from new except in the pretty blue color which wasn't an original color. However, if you use your tactile sense and feel the design inside the butter top, you will find it very sharply defined in the new; the knob on the new top is also very sharply defined whereas in the old, the knob is more smoothly formed.

NEW "CHERRY BLOSSOM"

Again, about ½" from the edge of the new top, you will notice one ring or band. In the old, there are two distinct indented rings or bands to be noted there. Unfortunately, there are several generations of these repros.

We could write a book on the differences between old and new scalloped bottom, AOP Cherry pitchers. The easiest way to tell the differences is to turn the pitcher over. Our old Cherry pitcher has nine cherries on the bottom. (This is not true for all pitchers!) The new one only has seven. Further, the branch crossing the bottom of our old Cherry pitcher looks like a branch. It's knobby and gnarled and has several leaves and cherry stems directly attached to it. The new pitcher just has a bald strip of glass halving the bottom of the pitcher. Further, the old cherry pitchers have a plain glass background for the cherries and leaves in the bottom of the pitcher. In the new pitchers, there's a rough, filled-in, straw-like background. You see no plain glass. (Our reproduction Cherry pitcher cracked sitting in a box by our typing stand — another tendency which we understand is common to the new!)

As for the new tumblers, the easiest way to tell old from the new is to look at the ring dividing the patterned portion of the glass from the plain glass lip. The old tumblers have three indented rings dividing the pattern from the plain glass rim. The new has only one. Further, as in the pitcher, the arching encircling the cherry blossoms on the new tumblers is very sharply ridged. On the old tumblers, that arching is so smooth you can barely feel it. Again, the pattern at the bottom of the new tumblers is brief and practically

NEW "CHERRY BLOSSOM"

nonexistent in the center curve of the glass bottom. This was sharply defined on most of the old tumblers. The pattern, what there is, on the new tumblers mostly hugs the center of the foot.

Several different people have gotten into the act of making reproduction Cherry Blossom. We've even enjoyed some reproductions of reproductions! All the items pictured on the previous pages are extremely easy to spot as reproductions once you know what to look for with the possible exception of the 13" divided platter pictured at the back. It's too heavy, weighing 2¾ pounds and has a thick, ¾" of glass in the bottom; but the design isn't too bad! The edges of the leaves aren't smooth; but neither are they serrated like old leaves. As with old glass, these new pieces vary over the years; so remember, it is BUYER BEWARE!

Now for a quick run-down of the various items.

The Cherry child's dishes were first made in 1973. First to appear was a child's cherry cup with a slightly lopsided handle and having the cherries hanging upside-down when the cup was held in the right hand. (This defiance of gravity was due to the inversion of the design when the mold, taken from an original cup, was inverted to create the outside of the "new" cup.) After we reported this error, it was quickly corrected by re-inverting the inverted mold. These later cups were thus improved in design but slightly off color. The saucers tended to have slightly off-center designs, too. Next came the child's butter dish which was never made by Jeannette. It was essentially the child's cup, without a handle, turned upside-down over the saucer and having a little blob of glass added as a knob for lifting purposes. You could get this item in pink, green, light blue, cobalt, gray-green, and iridescent carnival colors.

Two-Handled Tray — Old: 1⅞ lbs; ³⁄₁₈," glass in bottom; leaves and cherries east/west from north/south handles; leaves have real spine and serrated edges; cherry stems end in triangle of glass.

Two-Handled Tray — New: 2⅛ lbs; ¼" glass in bottom; leaves and cherries north/south with the handles; canal-type leaves (but uneven edges); cherry stem ends before cup-shaped line.

Cake Plate — New: Color too light pink, leaves have too many parallel veins which give them a "feathery" look; arches at plate edge don't line up with lines on inside of the rim to which the feet are attached.

8½" Bowl — New: Crude leaves with smooth edges; veins in parallel lines.

Cereal Bowl — New: Wrong shape, looks like 8½" bowl, 2" center.

Cereal Bowl — Old: Large center, 2½" inside ring, nearly 3½" if you count the outer rim before the sides turn up.

Plate — New: Center has smooth edged leaves, fish spine type center leaf portion; weighs one pound plus; feels thicker at edge with mold offset lines clearly visible on edge.

Plate — Old: Center leaves look like real leaves with spines, veins, and serrated edges; weighs ¾ pound; clean edges; no mold offset on edge.

Cup — New: Area in bottom left free of design; canal leaves; smooth, thick top to cup handle (old has triangle grasp point).

Saucer — New: Off-set mold line edge; canal leaf center.

NEW "FLORAL"
Importing Company out of Georgia

The big news in Floral is that reproduction shakers are now being found in pink, red, cobalt blue, and a dark green color. Cobalt blue, red, and the dark green Floral shakers are of little concern since they were never made in these colors originally. The green is darker than the original green but not as deep as forest green. The pink shakers are not only a very good pink, but they are also a very good copy. There are a lot of minor variations in design and leaf detail to someone who knows glassware well, but I have always tried to pick out a point that anyone can use to determine validity whether he be a novice or professional. There is one easy way to tell the Floral reproductions. Take off the top and look at the threads where the lid screws onto the shaker. On the old there are a pair of parallel threads on each side or at least a pair on one side which end right before the mold seams down each side. The new Floral has one continuous line thread which starts on one side and continues around the shaker until it ends above the beginning line on the other side. There is approximately one inch of overlapped thread making two lines for that inch; but the whole thread is one continuous line and not two separate ones as on the old. No other Floral reproductions have been made as of 2006.

NEW "FLORENTINE NO. 1"
Importing Company out of Georgia

Although a picture of a reproduction shaker is not shown, we would like for you to know of its existence.

Florentine No. 1 shakers have been reproduced in pink, red, and cobalt blue. There may be other colors to follow. We only have one reproduction sample, and it is difficult to know if all shakers will be as badly molded as this one. We can say by looking at this one shaker that there is little or no design on the bottom. No red or cobalt blue Florentine No. 1 shakers have ever been found, so those are no problem. The pink is more difficult. We are comparing this one to several old pairs from our shop. The old shakers have a major open flower on each side. There is a top circle on this blossom with three smaller circles down each side. The seven circles form the outside of the blossom. The new blossom looks more like a strawberry with no circles forming the outside of the blossom. This repro blossom looks like a poor drawing! Do not use the Floral thread test for the Florentine No. 1 shakers, however. It won't work for Florentine although these are made by the same importing company out of Georgia.

NEW "FLORENTINE NO. 2"

A reproduced footed Florentine No. 2 pitcher and footed juice tumbler appeared in 2000. First to surface was a cobalt blue set that alerted knowledgeable collectors that something was amiss. Next, sets of red, dark green, and two shades of pink began to be seen at the local flea markets. All these colors were dead giveaways as the footed pitcher was never made in any of these shades or hues.

The new pitchers are approximately ¼" shorter than the original and have a flatter foot as opposed to the domed foot of the old. The mould line on the lip of the newer pitcher extends ½" below the lip while only ⅜" below on the original. All of the measurements could vary over time with the reproductions and may even vary on the older ones. The easiest way to tell the old from the new, besides the colors, is by the handles. The new handles are ⅞" wide, but the older ones were only ¾" wide. That ⅛" seems even bigger than that when you sit them side by side.

The juice tumbler is not as apparent as the pitcher, but there are two major discrepancies as we examine them. The old juice stands 4" tall and the diameter of the base is 2⅛". The reproduction is shorter and smaller in base diameter. It is only 3¹⁵⁄₁₈" tall and 2" in diameter. These are small differences, we know, but color is the most significant difference!

NEW "IRIS"

New tumblers have two distinct differences. First, turn these upside down and feel the rays on the foot. New rays are very sharp and will almost hurt your finger if you press on them hard. Old tumbler rays are rounded and feel smooth in comparison. The paneled design on the new tumbler gets very weak in several places as you rotate it in you hand. Old tumbler paneled designs stay bold around the entire tumbler.

New dinner plates have two characteristics readily discerned from the old. The extreme edge of the pattern on the new dinners is pointed outward (upside down V). Old dinner plate designs usually end looking like a stack of the letter V, though optical illusions sometimes distort that a bit. Also, the inside rim of the new dinner plates slopes inward toward the center of the plate, whereas original inside rims are almost perpendicular and steeper.

Iris 6½" footed ice tea tumblers (new on left).

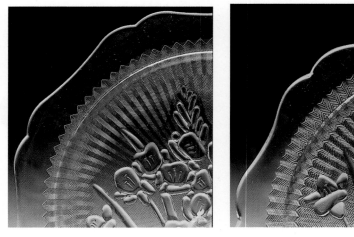

Iris dinner plate (new on left).

New flat tumblers (left) do not have herringbone in the pattern. There are many other minor differences, but that is the easiest to observe.

Iris coasters (new, thickened bottom at right).

NEW "MADRID"
Federal Glass Company, 1976 – 1977, 1980s, 1990s
amber, pink, crystal, blue, teal

New Madrid was introduced by Federal as "Recollection" in 1976 ostensibly for the Bicentennial. Each piece was dated '76 as shown here on a plate edge. The color was a deeper amber than the old.

The butter dish knob has mold marks running from north to south on the new; the mold marks run east to west on the old. I mention this only because on occasion new tops are "married" to old bottoms in an attempt to do a bit of "wool pulling."

Other items introduced in 1977 were candleholders, creamer and sugar with no lid, a footed candy and cover, a footed square bowl, and a footed cake plate. These last three footed pieces were not duplicates of the original Madrid. However, due to the first issue not selling so well, many stores failed to stock these latter pieces.

NEW "MADRID"

Indiana Glass issued "Recollection" glass in colors made originally. Instead of creating new collectibles in colors never made, they wiped out many a collector's dreams of financial profit by remaking glassware long discontinued. Shown above is the "new" Recollection Pink Madrid. Thankfully, not much pink was made in the 1930s when Federal made Madrid. The picture at the top shows new concepts in design that were never made. There are other pedestal pieces using the candlestick for the base besides the cake plate shown. Once you have seen the pale, washed-out pink on any of these items, you will never have trouble spotting these culprits.

Blue has been made in all of the pieces shown in pink. It is a vivid blue when compared to the older, subtle "Madonna Blue" shade made by Federal originally. The newest color is teal, which is a very greenish shade of blue.

NEW "MAYFAIR"

pink, green, blue, cobalt (shot glasses), 1977 onward; pink, green, "brownish" amethyst, cobalt blue, red (cookie jars), 1982; pink, red, cobalt blue (shakers), 1988; pink, cobalt blue (juice pitchers), 1993...

Mayfair cookie jars, at cursory glance, have a base which has a very indistinc design. It will feel smooth to the touch, it's so faint. In the old cookie jars, there's a distinc pattern which feels like raised embossing to the touch. Next, turn the bottom upside-down The new bottom is perfectly smooth. The old bottom contains a 1¾" mold circle rim that i raised enough to catch your fingernail in it. There are other distinctions as well; but that i the quickest way to tell old from new.

In the Mayfair cookie lid, the new design (parallel to the straight side of the lid) at the edge curves gracefully toward the center "V" shape (rather like bird wings in flight); in the old, that edge is flat, a straight line going into the "V" (like airplane wings sticking straigh out from the side of the plane as you face it head-on).

The green color of the cookie jar, as you can see from the picture, is not the pretty yellow/green color of true green Mayfair. It also doesn't "glow" under black light as the original green does.

The shot glass (which is hard to find in the original) has also been made in this patterm The green (totally wrong shade) and blue are no problem since the shot glasses have neve been found in these colors originally. The difficulty comes with the pink.

NEW "MAYFAIR"

Generally speaking, the newer shot glass has a heavier overall look. The bottom area tends to have a thicker rim of glass. Often, the "pink" coloring isn't right; it may be too light, it may be too orange. However, if these cursory examinations fail, there are other points to check.

First, notice the stem of the flower. You have a single stem in the new flower. At the base of the stem in the old glass, the stem separates into an "A" shape. Further, look at the leaves on the stem. In the new design, the leaf itself is hollow with the veins molded in. In the old glass, the leaf portion is molded in and the veining is left hollow. In the center of the flower, the dots (anther) cluster entirely to one side of the old design and are rather distinct. Nothing like that occurs in the newer version.

The juice pitchers shown below are photographed to show the bottoms. Note the original blue has a distinct mold circle which is missing on all reproduction pitchers. This and the oddly applied handles on the repros make these easily spotted!

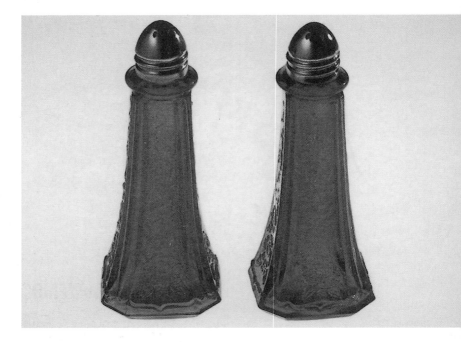

MAYFAIR SHAKER

	Old	**New**
Diameter of opening	3/4"	5/8"
* Diameter of lid	7/8"	3/4"
Height	4 1/18"	4"
Corner ridges on shaker	Rise 1/2 way to top then smooth out	Rise to top and are quite pronounced

* Most immediately noticeable factor.

NEW "MISS AMERICA"
Privately Produced 1977...
crystal, green, pink, ice blue, red amberina

The new butter dish in the Miss America design is probably the best of the newer products; yet there are three distinct differences to be found between the original butter top and the newly made one. Since the value of the butter dish lies in the top, it seems more profitable to examine it.

In the new butter dishes pictured, notice that the panels reaching the edge of the butter bottom tend to have a pronounced curving, skirt-like edge. In the original dish, there is much less curving at the edge of these panels.

Second, pick up the top of the new dish and feel up inside it. If the butter top knob is filled with glass so that it is convex (curved outward), the dish is new; the old knob area is concave (curved inward).

Finally, from the underside, look through the top toward the knob. In the original butter dish you would see a perfectly formed multi-sided star; in the newer version, you see distorted rays with no visible points.

Shakers have been made in green, pink, and crystal. The shakers will have new tops; but since some old shakers have been given new tops, that isn't conclusive at all. Unscrew the lid. Old shakers have a very neatly formed ridge of glass on which to screw the lid. It overlaps a little and has neatly rounded off ends. Old shakers stand 3⅜" tall without the lid. Most new ones stand 3¼" tall. Old shakers have almost a forefinder's depth inside (female finger) or a fraction shy of 2½". These vary as there are reproductions of the reproductions! Most new shakers have an inside depth of 2", about the second digit bend of a female's finger. (I'm doing finger depths since most of you will have those with you at the flea market, rather than a tape measure.) In men, the old shaker's depth covers my knuckle; the new shaker leaves my knuckle exposed. Most new shakers simply have more glass on the inside of the shaker — something you can spot from 12 feet away. The hobs are more rounded on most newer shakers, particularly near the stem and seams; in the old shaker these areas remained pointedly sharp!

New Miss America tumblers have ½" of glass in the bottom, have a smooth edge on the bottom of the glass with no mold rim and show only two distinct mold marks on the sides of the glass. Old tumblers have only ¼" of glass in the bottom, have a distinct mold line rimming the bottom of the tumbler, and have four distinct mold marks up the sides of the tumbler. The new green tumbler doesn't glow under black light as did the old.

New Miss America pitchers are all perfectly smooth rimmed at the top edge above the handle. All old pitchers that I have seen have a "hump" in the top rim of the glass above the handle area, rather like a camel's hump. The very bottom diamonds next to the foot in the new pitchers "squash" into elongated diamonds. In the old pitchers, these get noticeably smaller, but they retain their diamond shape. Only the non-ice lip pitcher has been reproduced!

211

NEW "MISS AMERICA"

The first thing you notice about the reproduced pieces is the extra dark, vivid cobalt blue color! It is not the soft cobalt blue originally made by Hazel Atlas. So far, only the cookie jar, juice, and water tumblers have been made as of 2006.

The original cookie jar lid has a mould seam that bisects the center of the pattern on one side, and runs across the knob and bisects the pattern on the opposite side. There is no mould line at all on the reproduction.

There are a multitude of bubbles and imperfections on the bottom of the new cookie jar that I am examining. The bottom is poorly moulded and the pattern is extremely weak. Original bottoms are plentiful anyway; learn to recognize the top and it will save you money!

As for tumblers, the first reproduction tumblers had plain bottoms without the four pointed design which makes these simple to distinguish. The new juice tumbler has a bottom design, but it is as large as the one on the water tumbler and covers the entire bottom of the glass. Originally, this design was very small and did not encompass the whole bottom as does this reproduction. Additionally, there are design flaws on both size tumblers that stand out. The four ribs between each of the four designs on the side of the repro tumblers protrude far enough to catch your fingernail. The original tumblers have a very smooth, flowing design that you can only feel. The other distinct flaw is a semi-circular design on the rim of the glass above those four ribs. Originally these were very tiny on both tumblers with five oval leaves in each. There are three complete diamond-shaped designs in the new tumblers with two being doubled diamonds (diamond shapes within diamonds); and the semi-circular design almost touches the top rim! There's at least 1/8" of glass above the older "fan."

Also, on the bottom of the tumblers, the four flower petal center designs in the old is open-ended leaving 1/8" of open glass at the tip of each petal. In the new version, these ends are closed, causing the petals to be pointed on the end.

NEW "SANDWICH"
Anchor Hocking Glass Company
crystal

At present, only the cookie jar has been re-introduced. The newer jar is much larger when compared with the old. To date, no other pieces have been made (2006)!

	Old	**New**
Height	10¼"	9¼"
Opening Width	5½"	4⅞"
Diameter/Largest Part	22"	19"

In recent years, Indiana Sandwich in amber, the smoky blue, green, and a sprayed red over crystal have been issued. In 1969 came red in quite a few pieces and these are difficult to tell from the older pieces of the 1930s. Any piece you see in amber or blue is of recent origin.

Bad news for collectors came in 1978 when Tiara announced that they were going to issue the Sandwich in crystal from decanter sets down to the domed butter dish. Our advice here is to be wary of paying any high prices for the old at this time. Since many of the original molds were used, there is little difference.

Green was made but it is a pale, washed-out green and will not glow under a black light as does the original green. Pictured at the top is the red decanter set and at the bottom is the teal butter dish which was a Tiara premium of the early 1980s. The wines shown in red are the earlier style. Those made in green and later in amber are shaped more like Iris cocktails.

NEW "SHARON"
Privately Produced 1976...
(blue, dark green, light green, pink, burnt umber, red, cobalt blue)

A blue Sharon butter turned up in 1976 and created a sensation. The blue was the color of Mayfair blue; but this color was unknown in the Sharon pattern. This fluke helped to quickly inform Depression enthusiasts that new editions were being made available.

In similar colors, you can distinguish between the old and the new butter dishes by noticing that the bottom ridge of the newer butter dish is sharply defined; the old bottom ledge is barely defined. Also, the top of the newer butter dish is heavier and thicker than the old — in most instances, it even weighs more. The knob is easier to grasp on the new butter dishes as it sticks up higher and you've more room to fit your finger around the knob and grasp the top. In the old butter dish tops, the knob fits so closely to the top that it makes it hard to grasp the knob.

In 1977 a "cheese dish" appeared having the same top as the butter. We put the name in quotes because it is but a parody of the original cheese dish. The new bottom of the dish is about half-way between a flat plate and butter dish bottom and is over thick, giving it an awkward appearance. The real cheese dish bottom more nearly resembles a salad plate with a raised rim. These "cheese dishes" are easily spotted as being new.

The newest reproduction in Sharon is a too light pink creamer and sugar with lid. They are pictured with their "Made in Taiwan" label. These sell for around $15.00 for the pair and are also easy to spot as reproductions. I'll just mention the most obvious differences. Turn the creamer so you are looking directly at the spout. In the old creamer the mold line runs dead center of that spout; in the new, the mold line runs decidely to the left of center spout.

On the sugar, the leaves and roses are "off" but not enough to describe it to new collectors. Therefore, look at the center design, both sides, at the stars located at the very bottom of the motif. A thin leaf stem should run directly from that center star upward on both sides. In this new sugar, the stem only runs from one; it stops way short of the star on one side. Or look inside the sugar bowl at where the handle attaches to the bottom of the bowl. In the new bowl, this attachment looks like a perfect circle; in the old, its an upside-down "v"-shaped tear drop.

As for the sugar lid, the knob of the new lid is perfectly smooth as you grasp its edges. The old knob has a mold seam running mid circumference. You could tell these two lids apart blind-folded.

While there is a hair's difference between the height, mouth opening diameter, and inside depth of the old Sharon shakers and those newly produced, We won't attempt to upset you with those 16th and 32nd of a degree of difference. Suffice it to say that in physical shape, they are very close. However, as concern design, they're miles apart. The old shakers have true-appearing roses. The flowers really look like roses. On the new shakers, they look like poorly drawn circles with wobbly concentric rings. The leaves are not as clearly defined on the new shakers as the old. However, forgetting all that, in the old shakers, the first design you see below the lid is a rose bud. It's angled like a rocket shooting off into outer space with three leaves at the base of the bud (where the rocket fuel would burn out). In the new shakers, this "bud" has become four paddles of a windmill. It's the difference between this ✷ and this ✷. The shakers wholesale for around $6.50 a pair.

A Sharon candy dish has been made by the infamous St. Louis group. It is very crude, thick, and should pose no problems. Be aware that it does exist and know your dealer.

NEW "SHARON"

Glossary

Amber — brownish yellow color (see Patrician photo for example).

Amethyst — a light, pastel purple as opposed to black amethyst which appears black until held to strong light whereby it shows deep purple.

Apricot — a dark yellow color, yet lighter in shade than amber; usually used to describe the darkest shade of Princess.

AOP — abbreviation for "all over pattern," usually used to describe Cherry Blossom.

Berry Bowl — term used by many glass companies to describe a round bowl.

Bonbon — a candy dish, usually uncovered.

Bread and Butter Plate — usually a 6" plate in a pattern that does not have a sherbet.

Cake Plate — a heavy, flat plate, usually having three legs.

Carnival — older, iridized glassware from early 1900s; also term used to describe the color of Floragold or an iridized pattern.

Celery — usually a long, narrow, flat dish; in Colonial, a two-handled dish taller than the sugar.

Cheese Dish — a covered dish, the bottom of which is normally flatter than that of the butter dish.

Chigger Bite — a term auctioneers use to describe a small chip on a dish.

Chop Plate — a large, flat plate called a salver by some companies.

Chunked — a polite way to describe a badly damaged piece of glass.

Claret — tall goblet of varying size depending upon company terminology.

Closed Handled — having solid tab handles.

Coaster — glass liner sometimes doubling as an ashtray.

Cobalt Blue — a deep, dark blue color (shown in Moderntone).

Comport/Compote — term used to denote small, open candy dish which is stemmed.

Glossary

Concentric Rings — circles within circles; gradually increasing or decreasing sized circles.

Console Bowl — centerpiece bowl, usually with candlesticks.

Cordial — small goblet of varying size depending upon company terminology.

Cracker Jar — term for what would be a modern-day cookie jar; they were sold with certain products packed inside them.

Cream Soup — a two-handled bouillon or consomme dish.

Decanter — usually a stoppered bottle for wine.

Delphite — a light blue opaque color; sometimes referred to as "blue milk glass."

Demitasse — a smaller than normal cup with saucer.

Domino Tray — a tray with a ring for creamer to reside in; the remaining surface within the tray being meant to hold sugar cubes.

Ebony — black color.

Etched — design acid engraved into glass; usually found on better quality glass.

Fired-On — color applied and baked on at the factory.

Flashed-On — color added over crystal; usually wears off as opposed to the fired-on color which does not wear off with use.

Flat — a non-footed dish; dish without a footed base or stem.

Fluted — scalloped edge.

Frog — heavy glass with holes for stem placement.

Goblet — a stemmed, bowl-shaped tumbler.

Gravy Boat — oval-shaped bowl used for serving gravy; often with a type of spout.

Grill Plate — a usually tri-sectioned plate of the type used in restaurants to keep the meat and vegetables divided from each other.

Hat Shaped — bowl looking like an up-turned hat.

Hot Plate — glass plate used for setting hot items on the table as a protection for the table or table spread.

Ice Blue — very light, crystal blue color.

Ice Bucket — a small bucket-like container for holding ice cubes.

Ice Lip — a guard or fold molded about the lip of a pitcher to keep ice from falling out into the glass when pouring from the pitcher.

Jadite — an opaque, light green color.

Jam Jar — small, covered jar for holding jam or preserves.

Luncheon Plate — usually an 8" or 9" plate, smaller than a dinner plate.

Mayonnaise — an open, cone-shaped compote or flat bowl with underliner.

Milk Glass — a white glassware, the color of milk, usually heavy.

Mold/Mould — a usually two-part encasement into which hot glass is poured and a glass object is formed; Depression glass was primarily glassware made from molds rather than being blown or formed by hand.

Monax — white color produced by MacBeth Evans, usually very thin.

Motif — the pattern or design on glass.

Mug — a heavy cup, usually flat bottomed.

Nappy — old word denoting a bowl.

Opalescent — white rimmed flowing into color.

Open Handled — handles having an opening for the finger or hand to reach through.

Parfait — a tall, ice cream dish of the type used for sundaes in soda fountains.

Pickle Dish — an oblong dish used for serving pickles; smaller than a celery.

Platinum Band — an applied silver colored rim on glassware.

Platonite — Hazel Atlas heat-resistant white glass often colored by a fired-on process.

Glossary

Platter — oblong or oval-shaped meat dish.

Preserve Dish — tall, footed dish often used as a candy.

Rayed — arrows or spoke-like designs on glass bottoms.

Relish — oblong dish, sometimes referred to as a pickle dish, often divided.

Rolled Edge — glassware having an edge curved out away from center.

Rope Edge — glassware with an edge having a rope-like design embedded in it.

Rose Bowl — small, curved-in edged bowl, usually having a small center hole and tri-footed.

Salad Plate — usually 7" – 7½" plate, for serving salads.

Salver — large, 11" – 12" non-handled serving plate.

Sandwich Server — a salver or sometimes a handled, often center-handled, serving plate.

Sherbet — small, usually footed, ice cream or dessert dish.

Teal — a blue-green color by all companies except Jeannette.

Tidbit — a two- or three-tiered serving dish made of increasingly smaller plates connected by a center metal pole, around 12"–15" tall.

Topaz — bright yellow colored glassware.

Trivet — a three-footed hot plate, usually about 7" in diameter, similar in design to three-footed cake plates but much smaller in diameter.

Tumbler — a glass.

Tumble-Up — a glass bottle with long neck having a small tumbler seated upside-down over the bottle neck serving as the bottle top; usually used on nightstand by bed.

Ultra-Marine — Jeannette's blue-green color.

Vaseline — a glowing yellow colored glassware similar to the color of the jellylike substance of the same name. If it looks green, then it is not vaseline.

Collectible Glassware from the 40s, 50s & 60s

8th Edition
Gene & Cathy Florence

Covering post-Depression era collectible glassware, this is the only book available that deals exclusively with the handmade and mass-produced glassware from the 40s, 50s & 60s. It is completely updated, featuring many original company catalog pages and 19 new patterns — making a total of 121 patterns from Anniversary to Yorktown, with many of the most popular Fire-King patterns in between. Each pattern is alphabetically listed, all known pieces in each pattern are described and priced, and gorgeous color photographs showcase both common and very rare pieces. 2006 values.

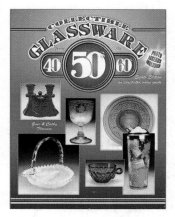

Item #6821 • ISBN: 1-57432-460-8 • 8½ x 11 • 256 Pgs. • HB • $19.95

Collector's Encyclopedia of Depression Glass,

Seventeenth Edition
Gene & Cathy Florence

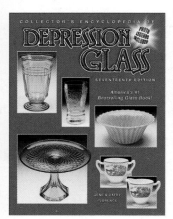

Since its first edition in 1972, this book has been America's #1 bestselling glass book. This completely revised seventeenth edition features the previous 133 patterns plus 11 additional patterns, to make this the most complete reference to date. Dealing primarily with the glass made from the 1920s through the end of the 1930s, this beautiful reference book contains stunning color photographs, vintage catalog pages, 2006 values, and a special section on reissues and fakes.

Item #6830• ISBN: 1-57432-469-1 • 8½ x 11 • 256 Pgs. • HB • $19.95

Schroeder's ANTIQUES Price Guide

now in FULL COLOR!

#1 BESTSELLING ANTIQUES PRICE GUIDE

▸▸ More than 50,000 listings in over 500 categories

▸▸ Histories and background information

▸▸ Both common and rare collectibles featured

only $17.95
608 pgs

celebrating our 25th EDITION

COLLECTOR BOOKS
P.O. Box 3009
Paducah, Kentucky 42002-3009
www.collectorbooks.com

APR 3 2007